D1074068

BASIC HISTORY OF
MODERN RUSSIA
Political, Cultural, and Social Trends

HANS KOHN

Professor of History
The City College of New York

E 70

AN ANVIL ORIGINAL
under the general editorship of
LOUIS L. SNYDER

D. VAN NOSTRAND COMPANY, INC.
PRINCETON, NEW JERSEY

TORONTO   LONDON

NEW YORK

To Robert Strausz-Hupé
in friendship and
fellowship

_____

D. VAN NOSTRAND COMPANY, INC.
120 Alexander St., Princeton, New Jersey (*Principal office*); 24 West 40 St., New York, N.Y.
D. VAN NOSTRAND COMPANY (Canada), LTD.
25 Hollinger Rd., Toronto 16, Canada
D. VAN NOSTRAND COMPANY, LTD.
358, Kensington High Street, London, W.14, England

All correspondence should be addressed to the principal office of the company at Princeton, N. J.

COPYRIGHT, ©, 1957, BY
HANS KOHN
Published simultaneously in Canada by
D. VAN NOSTRAND COMPANY (Canada), LTD.

Library of Congress Catalog Card No. 57-11307

PRINTED IN THE UNITED STATES OF AMERICA

PREFACE

RUSSIA has been a riddle to Europe for the last 250 years, attractive and luring as everything exotic and enigmatic is, and at the same time looked upon with suspicion and fear. Russia became a great European power at the beginning of the eighteenth century, but only at the beginning of the nineteenth century did she start to participate fully in the cultural and political life of the continent. By the beginning of the twentieth century there was great hope that Russia in the near future would take her rightful place as a full member of the European community of nations. The Russian Revolution, when it broke out in March, 1917, seemed to confirm this hope; eight months later the communist seizure of power destroyed it.

At that time contemporary Russia, rejecting many of the fundamental traits of Western civilization, emerged. It is still too soon for a historian to predict the course that contemporary Russia will take and what her final relationship with Europe will be. But present-day Russia can be understood only from a knowledge of the political, social, and intellectual conditions in which she was born. Modern Russian history—the Russia of the nineteenth century—assumes a unique place: it set the stage for the singular and decisive struggle between Russian traditionalism and modern Western liberty. Perhaps one day contemporary Russia will return to this struggle. It will be a good day for Russia and for the West. The present study proposes to set before the reader the context of the promises and perils which the history of modern Russia and its close relationship with Europe held for the future —promises and perils that in an altered form are still with us today.

Miss Elaine Day has been most helpful to me in the writing of this book. I certainly appreciate her always pleasant and cheerful cooperation.

HANS KOHN

3

TABLE OF CONTENTS

Part 1

MODERN RUSSIA

— 1 —

THE BEGINNINGS OF
MODERN RUSSIA

1. Divisions of Russian History. Western history
has been traditionally divided into ancient, medieval,
and modern history. Ancient history ended with the
downfall of the Western Empire and the decay of Roman civilization; the Middle Ages ended with the Renaissance. To the wide spaces in Eastern Europe inhabited
by the Slav-speaking peoples forming the Russian state,
these divisions are as inapplicable as they are to the Far
East. Russia never formed part of the Western Empire,
nor was it ever civilized from Rome; the great upheaval
of the Renaissance which laid the foundation for modern Europe did not touch Russia at that time. A more
fitting division for Eastern European and Russian history
has been suggested whereby the periods correspond to
the epochs in which various cities were the capital of
the Russian state—Kiev, Moscow, St. Petersburg, and
Moscow again.

The first Russian state originated about the end of the
ninth century around Kiev, where a Scandinavian dy-
nasty, founded by Rurik, ruled along the trade routes
from the Baltic to the Black Sea. This Russian state was
Christianized at the end of the following century from
Byzantium (Constantinople), the capital of the Eastern
Empire. Since then the Russian Slavs have followed the
Greek Orthodox faith. The invasion of Europe by the
Mongols or Tatars in 1237 destroyed the Kievan state.
From that time on, for almost three centuries, divided
into many small states under rulers of the Rurik dy-

9

nasty, Russia lived under Mongol domination. Finally, the great princes of Moscow succeeded in gathering in the Russian lands, in making themselves masters of all the various Russian principalities, in throwing off the Mongol yoke, and even in carrying Russian domination into Asia (Siberia) in 1582. In one hundred years Russian pioneers and conquerors had reached the Pacific shores and knocked at the gates of China.

This second Russian state which centered in Moscow laid the foundations for the extreme centralization of Russia. It believed itself to be the heir of the Mongol Khans and, as their successor, claimed suzerainty over Asia. Of even greater importance was its consciousness of being the legitimate successor to the emperors of the Eastern Empire after their capital, Constantinople, had fallen to the Turks in 1453. The ruling prince of Moscow married the niece and heiress of the last Byzantine emperor and assumed the title of Tsar (Caesar). From then on, Moscow claimed the dignity and title of the Third Rome and regarded itself as the seat of the (theoretically) universal empire and the center and guardian of the true (Orthodox) faith. Absolutism and centralization were inherent in the Mongol and Byzantine tradition, but Moscow developed them beyond any precedent. The immensity of the wide spaces entirely open toward the east seemed to demand centralization and absolutism as an antidote to centrifugal tendencies and growing anarchy. Liberty and diversity were sacrificed to the need of an overwhelmingly strong central authority which alone seemed capable of enabling Russia to expand eastward and westward and to establish its national power on an apparently unassailable basis.

The Rurik Dynasty died out in 1598, and in 1613 the Romanovs were elected Russian tsars. Alexei (1645-1676) started an organic and slow rapprochement with the West; his son, Peter the Great, a boy of four years at the death of his father and sole ruler in 1689, tried to speed this process far beyond Russia's capacity. In 1703 he moved Russia's capital from Moscow and its medieval and semi-oriental Kremlin to St. Petersburg, near the Baltic Sea where Western winds and ideas had easy access. When he died in 1725, Russia had modernized her armed forces to the extent of becoming a

serious competitor in the European power struggle. Yet
the foundations of Russian social, intellectual, and economic life remained largely antiquated and unaffected by
this military and technological transformation.

2. The Empire of St. Petersburg.   The third Russian state which centered in St. Petersburg lasted from
1703 to 1918 when Lenin reestablished Moscow as the
capital and inaugurated a new period of Russian history,
in many ways more similar to the first Moscow state
than to that of St. Petersburg. The Westernization of
Russia initiated by Peter the Great progressed slowly
throughout the eighteenth century; in 1726 the Petersburg Academy of Sciences was founded and in 1755 the
first Russian university in Moscow opened its gates to
students, though most of the instructors were, for the
time being, Germans. Catherine II (1762-1797) was
Peter's most successful and energetic successor; she carried on his military program of destroying the three
great realms that separated Russia from the heart of
Europe. Peter had destroyed the first of them—the
Swedish Empire—and established Russia firmly on the
Baltic Sea. Catherine destroyed the second of them—
Poland—and carried the Russian sphere to the Vistula.
She also took the first steps toward destroying the third
realm—the Turkish Empire—and by her conquest of
the Crimea, established Russia firmly on the Black Sea
and on the road to Constantinople. Her plans went fur-
ther: she hoped to expel the Turks from Europe and to
seat an Orthodox emperor again on the throne in Con-
stantinople. In expectation of this re-creation of the
Eastern Empire, she named her two oldest grandsons
Alexander and Constantine. But the Europeanization of
Russian life at large progressed little under Catherine.
(*See Readings Nos. 1 and 2.*)

Catherine's son Paul I, disliked and distrusted by his
mother, wished to undo many of her reforms. His foreign policy showed the lack of stability characteristic of
his personality. First, he turned against France, and the
brilliant Russian general Count Alexander Suvarov (1729-
1800) defeated the French revolutionary armies. Soon,
however, Paul cooperated with Napoleon and promised
to participate in the proposed conquest of British India.
Before Paul could carry through his plans, he was

strangled by court officers on the night of March 23,
1801. He was the last Russian tsar to die in this Oriental
fashion. Yet his death marked the beginning of modern
Russia; one of his few positive measures had been the
regulation of imperial succession according to the European system of primogeniture. Accordingly, his oldest
son Alexander, who had been involved in his father's
assassination, succeeded him.

3. Alexander I.   The new monarch, who ruled from
1801 to 1825, had received a superficial liberal education. As a boy he had been influenced by Frédéric César
de la Harpe (1754-1838), a disciple of the French
philosophes of the enlightened eighteenth century. Later
on, the Polish prince Adam Czartoryski (1770-1861)
was his companion; the two friends dreamt of the reform
of the over-militarized empire of which Alexander himself had written at the age of 19: "The affairs of state
are in complete disorder; graft and embezzlement are
everywhere; all departments are badly managed; order
seems to have been expelled from all parts of the country, but not withstanding all this the empire tends only
toward expansion." Yet despite these good initial intentions, Alexander, whose upbringing did not prepare him
for hard work or firmness of character, developed neither
the strength of mind nor the seriousness of purpose
which would have enabled him to end Russia's arbitrary
absolutism and to introduce a rule of law. He charged
the most promising Russian statesman of the period,
Michael Speransky (1772-1839), the son of a village
priest, with preparing a constitution for Russia after the
British model and a code of laws after the French
model. But a few years later, yielding to pressures from
his reactionary environment, Alexander dropped Speransky and his projects. The brief liberal period was over.
Alexander, who was a great charmer, especially of
women, and who liked to appear a man of benevolent
kindness, was neither trustworthy as a friend nor intelligent enough to face reality. With all his good intentions he accomplished nothing for Russia and did nothing to civilize her people. Napoleon, his great adversary,
in contrast, had no good intentions but left France immensely strengthened by his reforms of the French legal
and administrative systems.

4. Alexander and Napoleon.

The two men met on June 25, 1807, at the Niemen River which formed the frontier between Eastern Prussia and Russia. Both of them were conscious of their august position. Napoleon claimed the succession to the Roman Empire of the West, to Caesar and Charlemagne. Alexander knew himself to be the heir of the Eastern Roman Empire. Their starting points were different; Alexander had been born to the throne, whereas Napoleon had reached his exalted position through his own strength. Their armies had met twice before in war. In 1805 the Russians had been allied against France with Austria; in 1806, with Prussia. Both times the Russians had been decisively defeated. Now the two adversaries sought peace—as Hitler and Stalin were to do 132 years later—in their common hostility to England and in the vain hope that their combined armies could rule Europe and the world. The friendship between Alexander and Napoleon was, however, as uneasy as that between Hitler and Stalin. Their interests conflicted, above all, over the control of Poland and Constantinople. A war between Turkey and Russia was hardly terminated in May, 1812, when on June 24, Napoleon's armies crossed the Niemen in the direction of Smolensk and Moscow for the fateful invasion of Russia, which supplied the background for Leo Tolstoy's master novel *War and Peace*.

The Russian armies under the command of Mikhail Kutuzov (1745-1813) retreated before the invading French forces. After their defeat at Borodino, the Russians abandoned Moscow to the enemy. But the war had aroused the patriotism of the Russian masses. They made the cold vastness of Russia inhospitable to Napoleon, in whom they saw the anti-Christ, the representative of the hated West. Moscow was set afire and the retreating French armies were harassed by Russian partisans. Only pitiful remnants of the *Grande Armée* escaped the horrors of the Russian winter. The war has become known in Russian history as the Great Patriotic War. (*See Reading No. 3.*)

5. Alexander and Europe.

By Christmas, 1812, the invaders had been driven out of the Russian Empire. On New Year's Day, 1813, Alexander carried the war abroad to liberate Europe from Napoleon's yoke. In cooperation with Prussia, Austria, and Britain, Russian troops entered Paris and the Bourbon Monarchy was restored in France. The victors met at Vienna in 1814 to settle the fate of Europe. Alexander tried to expand Russia's frontiers deep into the heart of central Europe and to annex the whole of Poland, but the Western powers resisted this attempt. Alexander had to content himself with the larger part of Poland which included the capital of Warsaw. Poland's fate had weighed heavily upon the conscience of Europe since the three fateful partitions of that unfortunate and disorganized country at the end of the eighteenth century. Bowing to this deeply felt interest of Europe in Poland, Alexander granted the Poles a wide measure of autonomy and a constitution—the only liberal measure which he ever carried through. To his title of Emperor and Autocrat of all the Russias he added the title of King of Poland. The eastern parts of the former Polish state inhabited largely by a non-Polish peasant population and acquired by Russia in the first partition of Poland remained an integral part of the Russian Empire. For the next 150 years they formed a bitterly disputed area of conflict between the two Slav peoples, the Orthodox Russians and the Catholic Poles.

The Russian Empire emerged from the wars of the Napoleonic period with widely expanded frontiers. In addition to Poland, Russia acquired from Sweden in 1809 the Grand Duchy of Finland, which was allowed to preserve its enlightened Swedish civilization and an autonomous status, and from Turkey in 1812 the Rumanian province of Bessarabia. Many Europeans after 1815 feared that Russia would continue her expansion westward. Yet for one hundred years the western frontier of Russia remained, on the whole, remarkably stable; for in the nineteenth century—the most European period of Russian history—Russia, or at least its government, regarded itself as part of Europe and harbored no anti-Western aggressive plans. Russia's expansion during that time was directed to the east and the south. Under Alexander I, the Oriental Christian kingdom of Georgia on the eastern shore of the Black Sea was annexed in 1801, and the long-lasting war for the subjection of the freedom-loving Mohammedan mountaineers of the Caucasus started. Only in 1864 did the Russians succeed in "pacifying" them. The heroic resistance of the Caucasians, especially under the leadership of Shamyl (1791-1871), and the wild, rugged mountain scenery of the country inspired much of Russian romantic poetry. The two greatest Russian poets, Alexander Pushkin (1799-1837) and Mikhail Lermontov (1814-1841), drew part of their inspiration from their Caucasian experiences, and young Leo Tolstoy himself served as an officer in the Caucasian wars.

While Alexander was involved in wars on his Asian frontiers, he desired to face Europe as a champion of peace and Christian brotherhood. In 1815 he sponsored the Holy Alliance of the monarchs of Europe to whom he ascribed the firm determination of taking as their sole guide, both at home and in their relations with other states, the precepts of the Christian religion. In reality the Holy Alliance, which in international law hardly outgrew the status of a pious declaration, became the instrument for the cooperation of the three conservative military monarchies—Russia, Prussia, and Austria —against the rising liberalism of the West. In Europe, the leader of the alliance became the Austrian Chancellor Prince Metternich; Alexander represented its spirit in his guidance of Russia's internal development.

6. **Alexander and Russia.** After 1815, Alexander, the former liberal and European, turned more and more toward a Russian obscurantist mysticism. His empire, which claimed to be the political leader and the strongest power of Europe, left its few European visitors and diplomats with the impression of being un-European and backward in its administration, cultural life, and economic productivity. Alexander did nothing to remedy this condition during the last ten years of his reign. Haunted by the memory of the assassination of his father and of the frivolous life which he had led, he sought refuge in the Orthodox Church, to which he increasingly entrusted the supervision of all higher education in Russia. His foremost political adviser became Count Alexis Arakcheev (1769-1834), a brutal and narrow-minded soldier who had been the closest collaborator of Paul I. He introduced the system of "military settlements," an attempt to establish a thorough mili-

tarization of life in a "socialist" state in which individual dignity and all freedom of thought were unknown. In these darkening years of a career which had begun with much promise, Alexander I died suddenly in southern Russia on December 1, 1825. A persistent legend maintained that the emperor had not died but continued to live for many years as a saintly hermit in Siberia to expiate his sins. Whether he actually did is not known. Undoubtedly, however, he had left Russia, by his own fault, in a sorry state. The necessary steps for her overdue modernization and reformation as a member of the European community had not been taken.

7. Russia and Europe. But a number of young Russians, who during the campaigns in Europe had become better acquainted with Western civilization and liberty, were eager for such reforms. These young men were, in the large majority, scions of Russia's most distinguished noble families and officers in Russia's leading regiments. Their plans were vague. Russia had neither the social structure nor the intellectual traditions for the liberal constitution which they wished to force upon the government. They found themselves in an anomalous position, talking of Western liberty in a Russian environment. The situation was aptly described by the French ambassador to the Court of St. Petersburg in 1817, Count Antoine de Noailles: "The Russians are generally concerned with and seek in everything the superfluous without even having the necessary. They have an army, and an administration where corruption is pushed to the extreme degree; they bend under a yoke softened merely by the generous character of their master or by the right they arrogate to dispose of him if they dislike him; and in a state of society so remote from perfection and resembling in so many ways oriental governments, a young Russian officer, armed with his knout, subject of an absolute sovereign, surrounded by his own slaves, talks to you of the rights of peoples, of liberty, like a citizen of the United States."

The officers organized secret societies, of which the Northern Society followed a more conservative line and the Southern Society, in which Colonel Paul Pestel (1792-1825), son of a governor-general of Siberia, played a leading role, a more radical one. In both, lib-

eral trends mixed with nationalist aspirations. The death
of Alexander I and the confusion over the succession
to the throne between Alexander's two brothers—Constantine, who was the older but refused the throne, and
Nicolai—seemed to offer an opportunity for a military
uprising with the demand for the introduction of a constitution. The uprising took place on December 14, 1825,
but it was quickly suppressed by Nicolai, who had meanwhile ascended the imperial throne. The uprising in itself was a minor incident, yet it left deep traces in Russian history. Though the people remained entirely untouched, the educated upper classes sympathized with
the rebels; their harsh treatment at the hands of Nicolai
transformed them into legendary victims of autocracy
and into an inspiration for the Russian revolutionary
movement which dated its beginning to this "Decembrist"
uprising. Its memory made Nicolai I into a determined
enemy of all liberalism and a harsh upholder of autocracy. Five of the Decembrist conspirators, among them
Pestel, were executed; over one hundred were deported
to Siberia for penal servitude. Many submitted ignomin-
iously, showing before the autocratic power a humility
and repentance hardly compatible with the concepts of
Western individual dignity which they had professed.
But later on, some of those who were sent to doom or
exile displayed a fortitude which presaged a better future
for Russia.

The Decembrist uprising cast its shadow over the
whole era of the reign of Nicolai I, who came to the
throne at the age of 29 and ruled for thirty years. Like
his brothers, he showed interest primarily in military matters; though he was well educated and desired to improve
Russian administration, he rarely rose above the standards of a narrow-minded bureaucrat and a ruthless dis-
ciplinarian. Under his rule Russia was outwardly mighty
and powerful. Yet the Crimean War during which he
died in 1855 revealed autocratic Russia as a giant with
feet of clay. But the period was not without its glory:
in spite of a reactionary censorship and an obscurantist
educational administration, Russia made great cultural
progress under Nicolai I—not with the help of the government but in its self-assertion against it. The numeri-
cally small educated class, fertilized by its closer contact

with Europe, showed a remarkable vitality, though Western ideas could be only imperfectly assimilated into the
so different social and intellectual traditions of Russia.
The disparity between the European influences and the
Russian reality led to the frequent distortion, mostly in
an extremist form, of Western ideas. For the Russian
educated classes, alienated from their history and their
masses, reacted toward reality either with an extreme
skepticism or with a utopian faith—often with a strange
mixture of both. Sober critical thought had little influence upon modern Russia.

— 2 —

MODERN CULTURAL LIFE IN RUSSIA

1. The Policy of Nicolai I.   The regime of Nicolai
preserved a predominantly military character. High-ranking officers were placed at the head of many departments of state, including ecclesiastical affairs. The secret
police, organized as Section III in the imperial chancery,
exercised control over all aspects of Russian life. At the
same time the foundations of a government of law were
laid, though not observed, by the codification of the laws
of the Russian Empire (1835). The first steps were
taken toward the industrialization of the empire and the
creation of a middle class. The railroad from St. Petersburg to Moscow was built between 1843 and 1851. Technical schools were established. But little was done to deal
with Russia's most outstanding social problem, the condition of serfdom, under which the overwhelming part
of the population lived. Yet the long-suffering Russian
peasants did not accept their condition with good grace.
Peasant revolts were not uncommon and were always
suppressed with great severity. Hatred and fear on both

sides were also the heritage of the past. The memory of
the great peasant uprising under Emelyan Pugachev
which in the 1770's had devastated wide regions of southeastern Russia lived on. In its course, unspeakable cruelties were committed first by the peasants against the
landlords, and then in even greater ruthlessness by the
governmental forces against the peasants.

The autocracy of the tsar, the strict Orthodoxy of the
church, the serfdom of the peasants—these were regarded
as the secure foundations of Russian power and greatness, and were proclaimed as such by Count Sergei
Uvarov (1785-1855) who was Russia's minister of education from 1833 to 1849. To these three ancient pillars
of Russia a fourth was added—Russian nationalism,
which found its expression in an effort to Russify the
many non-Russian peoples which inhabited the Russian
Empire and were subject to its rule since the time when
the princes of Moscow started the ceaseless expansion
of Russian domination.

2. Education in Russia. Uvarov's educational
policy was directed at keeping "subversive" Western
ideas out of Russia. Travel between Russia and Europe
was made more and more difficult. Nevertheless, much
progress was made in the educational field. The University of Moscow became a center of intellectual fer-
ment, and some of its professors laid the foundations of
original research in Russia. Above all, there was an enthusiastic youth searching in the midst of Russian economic stagnation and bureaucratic maladministration for
new horizons. Important Western works were translated
into Russian; the knowledge of Western languages was
widespread among the aristocracy; the leading periodicals from France and Germany were eagerly read. The
number of students was still very small in comparison
to the population of the vast empire. The University of
Moscow counted 1,061 students; that of St. Petersburg,
379; in all the gymnasia, or secondary schools, throughout Russia there were only 17,800 students. Most of
these students came from noble families, though a few
were of the lower classes, mainly sons of Orthodox
priests.

Some of the professors followed the official line of
enthusiastic endorsement of Russia's unique greatness

and unimaginably grand future. The first incumbent of
the chair of Russian history at Moscow University,
Mikhail Pogodin (1800-1875), himself a self-made man
and the son of a serf, confessed in his writings to being
overwhelmed by the thought of Russia's wealth and
strength. "Who can compare with us? Whom will we
not force into submission? Is not the political fate of the
world in our hands whenever we want to decide it one
way or the other?" he wrote in 1837. "The untiring attention that follows every step of ours in Europe, that
incessant suspicion at our slightest moves, that muffled
grumbling of jealousy, envy and malice which issues
from newspapers and magazines, are they not the most
convincing proof of Russia's strength? Yes, the future
of the world depends on Russia—spoken so God wills.
What a glorious prospect!" Prince Vladimir Odoyevsky
(1803-1869) was at the same time convinced that "a
Russified Europe, as a new force, will bring life to
senile and decrepit Europe."

   3. Russia and Europe. Yet most of Russia's intellectual youth of the period did not share the official
optimism and arrogance about Russia's present and future status. They were indefatigably seeking a solution
to the Russian problem which to them appeared enigmatic and as full of portents as to those Europeans who
contemplated the Russian riddle. In endless discussions
throughout long nights these young intellectuals pon-
dered Russia's destiny: was she, or should she become,
part of Europe, or was she a world by itself with its
own peculiar character? Did Peter the Great's attempt
to Europeanize Russia open the way to her salvation or
to her destruction? Should Russia humbly learn from
the West or was she destined, by the strength of her
faith and her unity, to save Europe when the latter
foundered as a result of her national and class conflicts?
The answers to these questions was seldom given in a
clear-cut fashion. The Russian intellectuals frequently
changed their position, but on the whole, two great
schools of thought could be distinguished: that of the
Westerners—liberals who largely wished to follow the
example of Europe—and that of the Slavophils—nationalist romanticists who glorified the Russian past and ex-
tolled its imaginary virtues as superior to those of the

West, which they believed decadent. One of the leaders of the Westerners, Alexander Herzen (1812-1870), left in his memoirs, which he published under the title *My Past and Thoughts,* a remarkable picture of the intellectual fermentation in the Moscow youth of the 1830's and 40's.

The main influence on this youth was exercised in the 1830's by the German metaphysical philosophers Schelling and Hegel, and in the 1840's by the French socialists Saint Simon and Fourier. Among the leading Russian Westerners was, besides Herzen, Vissarion Belinsky (1811-1848), who became the first important Russian literary critic with a deep passion for improving Russian social conditions. It was largely through him that literature and literary criticism developed into the chief vehicles for voicing political and social demands in a country where all political activity and all social reform agitation were severely repressed. Belinsky was convinced that Russia's malady was rooted in "the lack of personal independence." Therefore, he concluded, "the government did not respect the individual, and the latter did not oppose the government. To the cynicism of the authorities corresponded the forebearing of the people. Russia's future will be a great danger to Europe and full of misfortune to herself if there is not (soon) an emancipation of individual rights."

Against the Westerners, the Slavophils, whose leaders were the theologian Alexei Khomyakov (1804-1860) and later the publicist Ivan Aksakov (1823-1886), maintained that the Russian national tradition contained the seeds not only of a true spiritual life but also of a just and charitable solution of the social question—above all of the agrarian problem. In her deep feeling of communal brotherhood Russia could find guidance in her own past and national character and did not have to learn from the West. On the contrary, Russia's historical character and her faith were intrinsically superior to the foundations of life in the West which were, the Slavophils proclaimed, in a state of disintegration and putrefaction as a result of the Western attitudes of violence, individualism, and destructive rationalism.

The debate between the Westerners and the Slavophils was stimulated by the challenging article of Peter Chaada-

yev (1794-1856) published in 1836. Therein he dared
to oppose the official glorification of Russia and to show
with a brutal outspokenness the retarded state of the
nation and its civilization. How could Russia, he asked,
a nation which had contributed nothing to the stream
of universal civilization claim the mission of guiding
Europe and mankind? Russia must first break her isolation, learn from Europe, and then—revitalized through
a growing union with the West—might one day catch
up with, and perhaps surpass, Europe. (*See Readings
Nos. 4 to 6.*)

4. **The Golden Age of Russian Literature.** Chaadayev may have been right about the sterility of Russia's
cultural past. He was certainly wrong with regard to the
Russia of his own time. Through contact with Europe,
Russian literature, which had been insignificant and un-
original at the end of the eighteenth century, suddenly
blossomed forth in the first half of the nineteenth century.
It immediately achieved a status of equality with the
other great literatures of modern Europe, first in poetry,
then in the novel. Vasily Zhukovsky (1783-1852), who
for a number of years was tutor to the future Tsar
Alexander II, created the new poetical language and
enriched the nascent Russian literature by many master-
ful translations from German and English poetry. Within
very few years he and some other gifted poets, like Constantine Batyushkov (1787-1855) and Pavel Katenin
(1792-1853), developed literary standards to a point at
which, very early in the history of modern Russian literature, its greatest master Pushkin could appear. Russians
as different in their tastes and political attitudes as the
Westernized novelist Turgenev, the fierce nationalist
Dostoevsky, and the Bolsheviks in power in 1937—the
centennial celebration of Pushkin's death—were unanimous in regarding Pushkin as the supreme glory of Russian letters. Though Pushkin was primarily a poet, two
of his long prose stories—*The Captain's Daughter,* a
story of the Pugachev uprising, and *The Queen of Spades*
—can give the Western reader a better introduction to
his work than the hardly translatable melodious sweep of
his poetry. His historical drama, *Boris Godunov,* has
become known abroad because of the opera made from it
by Modest Mussorgsky (1839-1881). It became the first

Russian opera to captivate the Western world when it was performed in Paris in 1908 with the great Russian basso Fyodor Shalyapin (1873-1938) in the title role. Yet of more lasting importance for Russian literature was Pushkin's *Eugene Onegin,* a novel in verse, whose two heroes became the models for many later Russian literary characters—Eugene Onegin, the self-indulgent dandy, a man as charming as he was weak, and Tatyana, whose noble morality and calm resignation evoked for her the love and admiration of many generations of Russian readers.

During Pushkin's lifetime two remarkable works marked the beginning of Russian theatrical literature. Alexander Griboyedov (1795-1829), who was implicated in the Decembrist uprising and who spent his short and romantic life as an officer and diplomat in the Caucasus and Persia, was the author of the first brilliant comedy in Russian, *Woe from Wit.* Mikhail Glinka (1804-1857) composed the first Russian opera *A Life for the Tsar* (1836), which glorified Russian patriotic deeds in defense against the invasion by Poland in 1613. Glinka's second opera *Russlan and Ludmilla,* which set to music one of the early romances written by Pushkin, never matched the popularity of the first. In the realm of poetry, Pushkin's mature work was continued by three men, very different in their art and in their lives—Alexei Koltsov (1809-1842), a master of lyrical folksongs; Fydor Tyutchv (1803-1873), a forerunner of symbolist poetry; and Mikhail Lermontov, the most truly romantic of his generation.

Whereas Russian poetry declined after 1840, the Russian novel began to emerge at that time to full stature in Nicolai Gogol (1809-1852). He has been regarded as the father of Russian realism. His play *The Inspector General,* his stories of which *The Overcoat* is the most famous and the most poignant, and his novel *Dead Souls* (1842), all present a great variety of pathetic characters representing the drabness and mediocrity of the Russian life of the period in such a way that Gogol appears often as a satirical critic of the backward and stagnant life under Nicolai I. But the weird and terrible reality which Gogol depicts was alive in him too, and therein he was the forerunner of Dostoevsky. He saw the whole desolateness of the Russia of his day and yet was deeply convinced of its unique and brilliant future. A tortured soul, Gogol died at the age of forty-two, having starved himself to death from religious fasting and from a profound melancholic depression which drove him to burn his unpublished manuscripts. Later Russian novelists inherited from Gogol his attention to detail and his introspective interest in character. Like him, they chose their subjects from contemporary Russian life, so much so, that the work of the great Russian novelists—Goncharov, Turgenev, Dostoevsky, and Tolstoy—can be used to illustrate the intellectual and social history of modern Russia.

It should be noted, however, that the personalities and situations with which the great Russian novel deals are in no way exclusively Russian. They unfold before us a picture of humanity in general; they throw light into the dark recesses of the human heart; they confront us with the predicament of modern man. But Russian literature, mirroring a society in transformation under the impact of modern Western ideas for which it was historically little prepared, highlights some of the perplexities of modern man more sharply than contemporary Western literature. This explains the great influence that Russian literature of the second half of the nineteenth century exercised upon the more advanced Western writers at the end of the century. This cultural interpenetration of Russia and the Western world belongs, however, to a later period than that of Nicolai I. During his reign the interpenetration was more political than cultural. It expressed itself, above all, in Nicolai's foreign policy.

— 3 —

RUSSIA'S ROLE IN EUROPE

1. The Gendarme of Europe. Nicolai tried not only to protect Russia from the danger of revolutionary ideas but also to secure throughout Europe the conservative order established at the Congress of Vienna. The maintenance of the status quo was Nicolai's fundamental policy, and he was willing to succor established governments threatened by internal upheavals. There was one point, however, where he did not follow this general line: Russian national interest in the weakening or destruction of the Turkish Empire conflicted with the international conservative interest of protecting the existing monarchies against the inroads of revolutionary nationalism.

Under Nicolai I Russia energetically continued her expansionist policy toward the southern shores of the Black Sea and across the Caucasian Mountains: her targets were the Turkish and Persian Empires, both even more obsolete and medieval than Russia. Russia's aggressive policy forced these two Islamic countries later to tread the road of Westernization and modernization and to gain new strength and cohesion through this transformation. But during the nineteenth century they owed their continued existence to the protection of Western powers, especially of Britain, who wished to prevent Russia from gaining control of the Straits of Constantinople, of the eastern Mediterranean, and of the Persian Gulf— the main strategic approaches to India. It was under Nicolai I, however, that Russia started to open up an inland road to India, inaccessible to British maritime opposition—a plan realized only under Nicolai's succes-

25

sor Alexander II. The inland route across the central
Asian deserts and oases of Turkestan brought Russia to
the frontiers of Afghanistan, which became a hotly disputed buffer between the British and Russian imperial
spheres. This Russian expansion to the south and south-
east and the diplomatic and military opposition which
it aroused were referred to in the nineteenth century
as the "Eastern" or "Oriental Question," a struggle for
the control of the Near and Middle East.

However, these strategic and imperial interests were
not the only issues which separated Russia and her chief
adversary Britain in the nineteenth century; the two countries were also frequently representing different or opposite political ideas: In the ideological struggle taking place
in Europe in the first half of the nineteenth century, Russia stood for absolutism and autocracy and England for
constitutional liberty and the rights of small nationalities.
This struggle found its most acute expression on Russia's
borders. As gendarme of a Europe based upon the divine
rights of kings, Nicolai suppressed the liberal and nationalist movements in Poland and Hungary, whereas the
sympathy of Western Europe went out to these two peoples in their struggle for national independence and constitutional liberty.

2. **Russia and Poland.** Paris, at that time the
center of revolutionary fire, fanned its flames throughout
continental Europe twice in the time of Nicolai's reign,
in 1830 and in 1848. When the July revolution of 1830
spread from France into neighboring Belgium and Germany, Nicolai was eager to send armed forces to put
down the revolution, but was unable to do so because he
was forced to extinguish the threatening flames much
closer to home in Poland. There, on November 29, 1830,
students and young officers tried to oust the Russian forces.
A provisional Polish government was formed in which
the conservative elements, ready for an understanding
with Russia, were originally in the majority but lost control to the radical elements in 1831. From February,
1831, the armed conflict raged throughout Poland. It
took the Russians seven months to regain control of the
country. Only in September, under the leadership of Field
Marshal Ivan Paskevich (1782-1856), who had distinguished himself in the campaigns against Persia and

Turkey, did the Russians reoccupy Warsaw. Paskevich became Viceroy of Poland; Poland's liberties were severely curtailed; a policy of Russification set in. The Polish national movement, however, continued in Western Europe where many Polish intellectuals and political leaders found refuge. The Western nations supported the Poles morally but shied away from military intervention in their behalf. Nor did the Western liberals then see clearly the fundamental shortcomings which precipitated Poland's downfall: the violent dissensions in the Polish ranks; the apathy of the Polish peasant masses who did not share the aspirations of the Polish upper classes; and the nationalist claims of the Poles to the eastern parts of the former Polish state with their non-Polish populations —a claim which united the Russians against the Poles and led Pushkin to publish some vehemently anti-Polish poems denying the West the right of interfering in Russian-Polish "family" affairs.

3. **Russia and Hungary.**   The wave of revolutionary unrest which spread from Paris in February, 1848, assumed infinitely greater proportions than that of 1830. This time not only a republic was proclaimed in France, recalling the fears of 1792-93; even the thrones in Vienna and Berlin were in danger of being overthrown by mounting public unrest. Only the most liberal government of the day and the most reactionary remained untouched by the European storm—Britain in the West, Russia in the East. Thus Nicolai could refer to his regime as an unassailable rock which by its power and quiet majesty would prove to be Europe's savior from "anarchy." The feeble attempts of freedom movements within Russia were easily suppressed. The Brotherhood of Cyril and Methodius which worked in Kiev for the cause of Ukrainian nationalism and the emancipation of the serfs, and the socialist circle formed by Mikhail Butashevich-Petrashevsky (1821-1866) in St. Petersburg, were crushed through the arrest of their members. Among the members of the Brotherhood was the Ukrainian national poet Taras Shevchenko (1812-1861), a former serf; among the Petrashevsky circle, the great Russian novelist Dostoevsky. Both were sent to Siberia; Shevchenko returned later shattered in health and spirit, while Dostoevsky returned as a man "converted" from a liberal into

an upholder of autocracy, Orthodoxy, and a chauvinist Russian nationalism. But Nicolai did not confine himself to dealing with the threat to his autocracy from within. In 1848 he moved his armies to act as the gendarme of autocracy outside the boundaries of his empire. First he set out against the Rumanian national movement whose aim was to unite and liberate the two Turkish provinces of Wallachia and Moldavia. In July, 1848, Russian troops, entering this time in agreement with Turkey, occupied the two provinces and easily restored order there.

Of greater importance for Russia and Europe, however, was the Hungarian revolution. There the Habsburg rulers were unable to put an end to the Hungarian striving for national independence. The Hungarian military forces were strengthened by the presence of a number of Polish émigrés, veterans of the Polish uprising of 1831, and among them General Josef Bem (1795-1850). Nicolai, afraid of the spread of the Hungarian revolution to Poland, was only too willing to support the Habsburgs. In June, 1849, a Russian army under Paskevich invaded Hungary. The Hungarians, weakened as the Poles had been by internal dissension and, above all, by their desire to establish their domination over non-Hungarian populations, surrendered in August. Many Hungarian and Polish refugees escaped to Turkey, among them General Bem and the Hungarian leader Lajos Kossuth. Russia and Austria demanded their extradition, but Turkey, supported by England, successfully resisted the request.

4. **Russia's Oriental Wars.** Russia's policy toward Europe was, under Nicolai I, defensive and conservative; against Turkey and Persia it was aggressive. In 1827 the Russian army under Paskevich defeated the Persians, and the city and territory of Erivan south of the Caucasus were annexed by Russia. In the following year the Russian armies invaded European Turkey, but obstinate resistance there slowed the Russian advance which reached Adrianople only in August, 1829, where in the following month a peace treaty was signed. Russia received possession of the mouth of the Danube, additional territories in the Caucasus, the rights of protection over Moldavia and Wallachia, and important commercial concessions. Though the treaty maintained the independence of the

Turkish Empire, it tended to transform it practically into a Russian protectorate. As Turkey's protector, Russia supported the Turkish sultan in his struggle against the insurrection of his Egyptian viceroy Mehemet Ali, who threatened to march on Constantinople.

In July, 1833, Turkey and Russia concluded the alliance of Unkiar Skelessi through which Russia tried to secure the recognition of her paramount interest in Turkey, a step which understandably aroused the distrust of the British government. Yet there were important Russian diplomats at the time who wished to avoid a break with England and tried to understand the West's misgivings. One of these diplomats, Baron Ernest Brunnow, pointed out in a memorandum in 1838 that Russian policy since the reign of Catherine II unfortunately justified only too well the suspicions concerning Russian intentions. "The English always remember," he wrote, "that the countries which were once under the protection of Russia have all ended by losing their independence; that Russia has extended her protection to Poland in order to bring about her partition; that she has freed the Georgian tribes from the Turkish dominion and has subjugated them; that she has recognized the independence of the Crimea to annex it to her empire. Examples of the past, therefore, hamper the present, and the noble motives of our policy today are denied because memories of distant events are still alive in the minds of foreign governments who are alarmed by and envious of our might."

5. The Crimean War. The convention of 1841, signed by the five European great powers and regulating the regime governing the Straits of Contantinople, brought a temporary relaxation in the continuing tension over the Oriental or Eastern Question. But the short respite ended in 1852 when the new French government of Louis Napoleon officially assumed the protection of Roman Catholic rights in the Holy Land and these rights conflicted with those of the Greek Orthodox Church protected by the Russian emperor. The Turkish sultan gave in to French wishes and rejected a Russian ultimatum asserting the tsar's paramount interests. As a result, a Russian army invaded Moldavia and Wallachia in 1853 while a strong Anglo-French fleet supported Turkey by anchoring at the entrance of the Dardanelles. After long and confused diplomatic negotiations, open hostilities broke out in October, 1853. Britain and France now became Turkey's official allies while Russia was bitterly disappointed in not receiving any help from the two other eastern monarchies, Prussia and Austria. In fact, Austria proclaimed her armed neutrality which factually supported the Allies. She then moved her armies into Moldavia and Wallachia after the retreat of the Russian troops. The British and French forces were joined by the Kingdom of Sardinia, the nucleus of the future united Italy. Thus the Russians faced a strong coalition. They not only complained of Habsburg "ingratitude," but the Slavophils saw in the war an aggression of the united West against Orthodox Russia in support of "infidel" Turkey.

The military operations themselves hardly corresponded to the claims of what seemed a major conflict in the light of diplomacy. The Western powers were ill-prepared and did not establish an efficient united command. In September, 1854, British, French, and Turkish troops landed on the Crimean peninsula in order to capture the great Russian naval port of Sevastopol. From this principal battleground the war became known as the Crimean War. The stubborn defense of the fortress of Sevastopol rightly has become celebrated in Russian literature and history, partly thanks to the tales of Leo Tolstoy who as a young officer participated in the war. In spite of some conspicuous Allied victories in the battles at Balaklava—a battle well known in English-speaking lands by the ill-fated and ill-directed charge of the British light cavalry—and at Inkerman, their armies suffered heavily through illness and an appalling lack of proper medical facilities. Only on September 9, 1855 could the Allies take possession of what remained of Sevastopol. (*See Reading No. 7.*) At the beginning of the following year a peace congress convened in Paris. It ended the war without any territorial loss for Russia and with the guarantee by all powers of the independence and territorial integrity of Turkey. But the Russians felt profoundly aggrieved by the provision which declared the neutralization of the Black Sea; it was at all times to stay open to the commercial vessels and be closed to men-of-war of all nations.

The Crimean War had an importance far beyond its military operations. It destroyed the legend of Russia's invincibility and gigantic strength. The effect of this revaluation on Russia's development was thoroughly salutary. Like all the wars in which Russia in modern times was defeated, the Crimean War became the incentive for domestic reform and for the inauguration of a more liberal regime. In the same way, the growth of Russian freedom and a true modernization were stimulated in 1905 after Russia's defeat in the war against Japan, and in March, 1917, when Russia was defeated by Germany. Russia's great victorious wars, on the other hand, like the war against Napoleon in 1812 and the war against Hitler in 1945, led to a tightening of Russian autocracy and to a determination to abandon all incipient liberal reforms. But the Crimean War, during which Nicolai I died and his son Alexander II ascended the Russian throne, marked the beginning of a new and hopeful era in the difficult history of liberty in Russia's government and life and of a closer intellectual and cultural intercourse with Europe, and even America. (*See Reading No. 8.*)

— 4 —

THE FIRST LIBERAL PERIOD

1. The Emancipation of the Serfs. Defeat in the Crimean War convinced Russia's leading circles that reform was necessary. Yet these reforms, though of fundamental importance, remained half-hearted concessions on the part of the government and of the nobility. No step was taken to curtail the autocracy. Thus the regime of Alexander II which started with great expectations finally fell very short of the hopes of even the moderate

liberals. From several years of protracted negotiations on
the part of the nobility and the bureaucracy, among
whom were many opponents of emancipation, the
statute of March 3, 1861, finally emerged. It established
the civil liberties of the serfs, but it did not solve the
question of the ownership of the land to the satisfaction
either of the peasants or of the former landowners. The
peasants had always regarded as their own the land on
which they worked as serfs; they were bitterly disappointed in receiving only part of the land, and for this
part they ,were forced to pay the former landowner frequently excessive compensation in installments over
originally forty-nine years. Some temporary work "obligations" to be rendered the former masters burdened the
peasants for a number of years. The terms surrounding
the allotments of land to the former serfs were of utmost
complexity. Frequent amendments and cumbersome conditions caused tenure and payments to be insecure for
several years.

This famous emancipation act which earned Alexander II the title of "Tsar-Liberator" did not establish
the peasants as free farmers in the Western sense of the
word. They remained organized in communal groups or
land communes, called *obshchina* or *mir*. (*See Reading
No. 9.*) This village commune continued to be treated,
for fiscal and police purposes, as an entity. Though the
former serf was no longer dependent upon the landowner,
he remained dependent upon the village commune. The
joint responsibility of the village commune was abolished
only in 1903; corporal punishment for peasants lasted
until 1904; and only after 1906 were the several restrictions imposed upon the freedom of the peasants relaxed.
The Slavophils looked favorably upon the village communes as a traditional Russian institution preserving the
social order and mutuality. Westerners, on the other
hand, regarded the commune as an obstacle to the
growth of individual initiative and, therefore, of economic
progress and political education. (*See Reading No. 10.*)

The emancipation of the serfs forced the introduction
of new governmental organs. Formerly the administrative, judicial, and police functions had been exercised
by the landowners. Now the local self-government, first
instituted in a very imperfect form by Catherine II, was

somewhat modernized. The bodies of local self-government—the *volost,* or group of village communes, and
the more important *zemstvo,* as the district and provincial
assemblies were called—were greatly restricted in their
autonomy, which in the case of the *zemstvo* covered
roads, public health, charity, and agriculture, and were
strictly supervised by government officials. Some Russian
liberals hoped that the *zemstvos* would provide an education in self-government and form the basis for future
constitutional developments. Municipal councils called
dumas were established in the cities. More important and
more beneficial was the institution of an independent
judiciary which ended the previous corruption for which
Russian courts had been notorious. In 1874, finally, universal military service created a more modern army, re-
placing a standing army in which the usual term of
service ran to twenty-five years. (*See Reading No. 11.*)

2. **Liberalism in Education and the Arts.** The beginning of Alexander's regime led to a relaxation of censorship. In 1857 Herzen founded the first free Russian
newspaper *Kolokol (The Bell)* in London. Many copies
were smuggled into Russia and widely read even in the
highest circles. Protests against corruption and abuses
inside Russia could be effectively voiced through *Kolokol.*
But even in Russia, periodicals and books could appear
without being submitted to preliminary censorship. The
universities received a greater autonomy. New secondary
schools were opened and made accessible to students
of all classes, and the *zemstvos* received the right to
widen the net of elementary schools. Yet these modest
good beginnings were partly undone when in 1866 Count
Dmitri Tolstoy (1823-1889) became Minister of Education, a position which he filled for fourteen years con-
jointly with the Chairmanship of the Holy Synod, the
chief ecclesiastical body of the Russian Church. A bigoted
reactionary, Count Tolstoy was determined to crush
academic freedom and liberty of thought, and his coercive
measures were met with a growing restlessness and revolutionary zeal among the students.

Nevertheless, learning and the scientific spirit made
much progress under Alexander II. The Europeanization
of Russian life was carried a considerable step forward.
Vassily Klyuchevsky (1841-1911), the son of a village

priest, became the leading Russian historian. For many years he occupied the chair of history at the University of Moscow. His main work, *Lectures on Russian History,* analyzed in four volumes the social trends in Russia from the beginning to 1762, the year in which Catherine II ascended the throne. A well-known chemist, Dmitri Mendeleev (1834-1907), taught biology at Odessa before he emigrated to Paris where he became Louis Pasteur's successor as director of his Institute. The great physiologist Ivan Pavlov (1849-1936) belongs to a somewhat later generation. But more important than the appearance of a few prominent scientists was the rapidly growing veneration among the Russian academic youth for the natural sciences and their technological application. This young generation was filled with a boundless admiration for the potentialities of modern science, an admiration not yet matched by actual knowledge or correlated to the social environment. This utopian reliance on a science interpreted in the sense of generalized and overblown European doctrines—German materialistic philosophy, French socialism, and English utilitarianism and positivism—was coupled with a total rejection of the existing Russian tradition and society and of the lasting moral and esthetic values underlying Western civilization.

These young materialists have become known as "nihilists," a name given by Ivan Turgenev to the spokesman of that generation, the student of medicine Bazarov, in his novel *Fathers and Sons* (1861). Bazarov was convinced that "every single convention of our present day existence, in family or social life, calls for complete and ruthless rejection." These young nihilists turned materialism into a kind of dogmatic theology, anticipating therein the twentieth century communists. In endless debates they asked themselves the question, "What to do?" Their recognized leader was Nicolai Chernyshevsky (1828-1889), the son of a priest. While imprisoned in the St. Petersburg fortress, Chernyshevsky in 1863 wrote a novel *What to Do?* which, though without any artistic merits, became the bible of the Russian radical youth and was highly esteemed by Lenin. Chernyshevsky's younger contemporaries, Nicolai Dobrolyubov (1836-1861) and Dmitri Pisarev (1841-1868), became the leaders of the

new literary criticism which was remarkable for its re-
pudiation of the esthetic element in literature and the
arts. According to them, all cultural activities were to
serve exclusively utilitarian social ends. Pisarev characteristically called one of his essays *The Annihilation of
Aesthetics*. Russia and mankind stood much more in need
of good cobblers than of great painters or writers, so
they believed. Literature to these critics had to be, as it
is called today, "engaged" literature, an instrument in
the social and political struggle.

3. **The Superfluous Man.** This radical devotion of
the young generation to material activity and even to
activity at any price can be explained as an extreme reaction to the stagnation of Russian life and the verbose
idealism of the older generation. The heroes of many
Russian novels of the period were weak and vacillating
men who suffered from a feeling of frustration. Self-
centered and self-pitying, they lacked will power and energy. Pushkin's Eugene Onegin was a first anticipation
of this type in the mood of a Byronic romanticism. Lermontov intensified the self-destructive trends of the proud
dandy in Petchorin, the hero of his novel *A Hero of Our
Time* (1839). Sweeter and more melancholy are the
similar characters which the great novelist Ivan Turgenev
(1818-1883) presents to us in most of his works. It was
Turgenev who, in one of his early tales called *The Diary
of a Superfluous Man*, introduced the name which was
then applied to a whole line of similar "heroes." The central figure of Turgenev's novel *Rudin* (1855) is a typical
"man of words but not of deeds," and so is Nezhdanov
in his last novel *Virgin Soil* (1876). Most of these men
are contrasted, as already Eugene Onegin was, with
young women of unusual strength and integrity of character who show greater purity and dedication and more
practical common sense than their male opposites.
Chivalry and the idealization of women had been prac-
ticed in the West since the Middle Ages. In Russia they
were unknown until the nineteenth century when they
suddenly became central themes of the Russian cultured
class.

The most famous realization of the "superfluous man"
was Oblomov in the novel by that name (1857) by Ivan
Goncharov (1812-1891). "Oblomov is more than a

character, he is a symbol," D. S. Mirsky wrote. "He obviously was, and was immediately recognized to be, the embodiment of a whole side of the Russian soul, or rather of a side of the soul of the Russian gentry —its sloth and ineffectiveness. He has a high sense of values. He is open to generous aspirations but incapable of effort or discipline." Though Oblomov means well and arouses the sympathy of the author and the reader, the story ends in an atmosphere of inevitable doom gradually descending upon Oblomov. The novel appeared on the eve of the emancipation of the serfs, an event which doomed the old stagnant genteel order and brought a new youth to the fore, who were no longer members of the landowning nobility but often the sons of village priests, of former serfs, and of the rising middle class. These young men were determined to put an end to the old order and to its superfluous man.

4. The Great Russian Novel. The period of Alexander II with its somewhat freer intellectual life witnessed the flowering of the great Russian novel and of its three masters, Turgenev, Fyodor Dostoevsky (1821-1881), and Count Leo Tolstoy (1828-1910). Each one was different in his personality and art. Turgenev and Tolstoy were the sons of aristocratic landowning families; Dostoevsky grew up in the dismal quarters of Moscow and never had the poetical sense for the beauties of nature in which the two others excelled. Turgenev's talent was more lyrical and emotional; Tolstoy was a master of broad epic descriptions; and Dostoevsky constructed his novels as dramatic plays with a climax of effects. In Dostoevsky's books incessant and self-revealing conversations took the place of that minute characterization from without, from which much of Tolstoy's strength was derived.

These writers were as different in their political views as they were in their art. Turgenev was a decided friend of the West and of Western civilization; he spent most of his life in Paris where he was a close friend of Gustave Flaubert and Henry James. Dostoevsky and Tolstoy both rejected Western civilization, though in a very different way. Tolstoy, a nineteenth-century disciple of eighteenth-century Rousseauism, found Western civilization artificial and mechanized. A religious man in the eighteenth-

THE FIRST LIBERAL PERIOD

century sense of the word, he was an optimistic humanist.
He turned to nature and to natural man whom he found
best embodied in the good and primitive Russian peasant.
Dostoevsky, on the other hand, was pessimistic about
human nature and deeply probed the perversion and
sinfulness of the human heart. In this way he was a
much more "modern" writer than was Tolstoy. Dostoevsky had a mystical trust in the goodness of the simple
Russian folk, not so much as simiple folk but as Russian
folk. He was an extreme Slavophil who regarded the
Russians as the truly god-bearing people. In his fierce
Russian nationalism he hated Western civilization and
felt profoundly unhappy during his sojourn in Europe.
It should be added that Dostoevsky's personality can be
partly explained by his unhappy personal experiences,
both in his youth and in his later years when, as a political prisoner, he underwent the horrors of hard labor
in Siberia and of the life of a private soldier in a distant
Siberian garrison under the oppressive conditions of the
period. While Tolstoy was an embodiment of physical
health, Dostoevsky was throughout his life a sickly man,
suffering until the last fourth of his life from epilepsy,
miserable poverty, unhappy love affairs, and an unfortunate marriage. It was partly from his own experiences
and his own character that he created unforgettable por-
traits of suffering and humiliated mankind, of sin and
contrition, of religious doubt, and of longing for the certainty of salvation.

Of Turgenev's novels, two—*Rudin* and *Fathers and
Sons*—have already been mentioned. The rights of the
individual were paramount with Turgenev as with no
other Russian novelist. Litvinov, the hero of the novel
Smoke, is one of those pioneers of Western civilization
who, according to Turgenev, were the hope of a new
Russia which would correspond neither to the revolutionary dreams of the radicals nor to the reactionary yearn-
ings of the conservatives. Turgenev preferred gradual-
ness from below under the guidance of enlightenment
rather than violence, whether the latter came from below or above. In his last novel *Virgin Soil* (1876), the
silent, practical and conscientious factory manager represented a more advanced development of the type introduced a decade earlier in Litvinov. Of the period of

transition in which Turgenev and his heroes lived, he wrote: "The new was accepted reluctantly, the old had lost all its strength; the bungler clashed with the un-scrupulous; all the shaken life was quaking like a marsh, and only the one great word Freedom hovered like the divine spirit above the waters. Patience was required most of all, and patience not passive, but active." Tur-genev never penetrated as deeply into the possible per-versions of the revolutionary spirit as did Dostoevsky in his novel *The Possessed* (1871), a bitter attack on "godless" socialism. It is one of the four great novels on which Dostoevsky's world fame rests; the others are *Crime and Punishment* (1866), *The Idiot* (1868), and *The Brothers Karamazov* (1880). In Prince Myshkin, the "idiot," and in Alyosha, the youngest of the brothers Karamazov, Dostoevsky tried to create representatives of an ideal Russian Christianity; they are, by far, less successfully drawn than his more complex and tragic characters of revolted intellectuals, like the student Ras-kolnikov in *Crime and Punishment* and Ivan Karamazov.

The frequently morbid and intensely tormented char-acters of Dostoevsky contrast sharply with the more serene atmosphere which pervades Tolstoy's novels with their confidence in the forces of nature and life. Through the vivid scenes of the horror of battle in *War and Peace* there, nevertheless, shines a light of consolation and happiness, and the novel has been rightly called the "heroic idyl" of the Russian nobility, a class with which Tolstoy identified himself. More tragic is the atmosphere in his later novel *Anna Karenina* (1877). The new at-titude toward life which emerged in that novel, an atti-tude far less optimistic and more puritan than that pre-vailing in his former creations, led to the religious crisis which, after 1879, brought him to place his great art at the service of morality. Even then he wrote outstanding works of literary art like *The Death of Ivan Ilyich* (1886) and his last novel *Resurrection* (1899), but he became better known in his later years for his political philoso-phy which can be summed up as a religious anarchism that rejected all forms of violence and compulsion whether backed by the authority of the state or of the church. He was an extreme pacifist, and though as a pacifist he could not support the violence of the revolution, he courageously opposed the persecutions of the revolutionaries by the government, and his mighty voice rang out again and again from his country estate, Yasnaya Polyana, in defense of many moral causes.

5. **Russian Music.** Whereas Russia did not excel in the visual arts, music flowered under the influence of the contact with Europe as suddenly as did literature in the nineteenth century. The Russian Music Society, which was founded in 1859 and in the following year established conservatories in St. Petersburg and Moscow, was active in sponsoring orchestras and concerts and in raising the musical level throughout the country. It was helped in its effort by Russia's first world-famous virtuoso, a pianist and prolific composer, Anton Rubinstein (1829-1894), whose brother Nicolai became the first director of the Moscow Conservatory. Original Russian music after Glinka owes its importance to a group of composers, all active in the 1860's, known as "The Five" (*Kuchka*). None of them started as professional musicians; all of them were fervent nationalists and wished to create a "realistic" music based on Russian folk traditions. Cesar Cui (1835-1915), the son of a Frenchman and later a general in the Russian army, was the least nationalistic of the five. Alexander Borodin (1833-1887), a busy professor of chemistry and founder of a school of medicine for women, wrote fascinating music of bold melodies; his opera *Prince Igor,* left unfinished at his sudden death, was completed by Nicolai Rimsky-Korsakov (1844-1908), originally a naval officer who, while serving at sea, wrote the first Russian symphony. He had a vivid sense of orchestral color, akin therein to the French composer Hector Berlioz. Mily Balakirev (1837-1910) established the Free School of Music in St. Petersburg, the center of the new nationalist music. The most original of the five was Modest Mussorgsky (1839-1881), who started his career as an officer in the guards. He had little musical training and his life was shortened by drunkenness and drug addiction, but his work marks the culmination of musical realism in Russia. Better known abroad than any of these five is Peter Tschaikovsky (1840-1893), who studied music under Anton Rubinstein. Though he was not a nationalist, his music was typically Russian in its sensitive expressiveness. His sym-

phonies, especially the sixth called *Pathétique,* have been
performed all over the world.

6. **The Genesis of the Revolutionary Movement.**
Although freedom of the press was not realized under
Alexander II and political parties were not allowed to
be formed, public opinion became for the first time a
factor influencing the Russian government. Liberals
pleaded for constitutional reforms, whereas the conservatives led by Mikhail Katkov (1818-1887) upheld the
autocracy and praised its virtues. Katkov was a gifted
journalist who, as editor of the *Moskovskie Vedomosti*
(*Moscow News*), preached an extreme and aggressive
nationalism. He was one of the moving forces behind
Russian Pan Slavism, which was a movement striving
not only to unite all the Slav peoples under Russian
leadership but also to impose upon them the Russian
culture and language. In its extremist form the movement never found favor with the other non-Russian Slav
peoples and was bitterly opposed by the Poles. The conservative and nationalist trends were strengthened by the
Polish insurrection of 1863 which climaxed several years
of unrest under the administration of the Marquis Alexander Wielopolski (1803-1877), a proponent of Russian-
Polish cooperation. Like the Polish uprising in 1830,
that of 1863 was poorly organized and poorly led, yet
the Poles fought with great courage despite the striking
discrepancy between the numbers and equipment of the
forces opposing each other. European sympathy was
again heartily with the Poles, and the Western governments tried to intervene on their behalf, but their intervention was sharply rejected by the Russians, and the
West refused to go beyond verbal protests and passive
manifestations of sympathy—partly because Prussia under Bismarck sided with Russia. Thus the uprising was
liquidated and the last vestiges of Polish autonomy were
abolished. Though the Polish peasants were generously
treated by the Russian administration in order to establish a counterweight against the Polish nobility, the ruthless Russification of Poland, where Russian became the
language of instruction in all schools, solidified Polish
national consciousness and awakened a Polish national
feeling among the peasants.

The era of Alexander II witnessed also the beginning

of the revolutionary movement, which was no longer carried on by secret societies of officers as it was before 1825. It now found a broader basis of support, not among the people in general but among intellectuals and students. The extremist theories of the anarchist Mikhail Bakunin (1814-1876) and of nihilist agitators who believed in violence in disregard of all accepted morality, such as Sergei Nechaev (1847-1882) and Peter Tkachev (1844-1885), influenced the beginnings of the revolutionary movement and were later revived in Leninism. Nechaev organized the cold-blooded murder of his fellow-revolutionary Ivan Ivanov in 1869, a crime story which was used by Dostoevsky as the plot of his novel *The Possessed.* Tkachev argued that backward Russia was ripe for a socialist revolution as soon as a closely knit, determined and armed small minority was able to seize power and to impose its will. All these early leaders of the revolutionary movement were—in sharp distinction from Herzen who learned to understand the value of ordered liberty while he lived in England—strongly anti-liberal and anti-democratic. The parliamentary and reformist traditions of the West were unknown in Russia.

Meanwhile among the youth in Russia many placed their hope in the peasants—"communists by instinct and by tradition"—and in their communal institutions. The youth decided to go to the people (*narod*) to enlighten and arouse them; thus the movement became known in Russia as *narodnichestvo,* or populism. The mood and attitudes of its adherents were described by Turgenev in some of his novels, especially in *Virgin Soil.* The most important secret organization of the movement was called *Zemlya i volya* (1862). The name expressed the program: the word *zemlya* (land) meant all land to the peasants; the word *volya* signifies liberty unhampered by Western constitutional limitations. At the same time *volya* means "will, a determined effort." Many of the *Narodniki,* or populists, originally believed in a spontaneous action by the Russian people and its allegedly deeply inherent socialist instinct. But subject to severe governmental repressions, and despairing of reaching their aims by underground education and propaganda, some of the Russian youth, among them several dedicated women, turned to revolutionary terror. Many of them committed their political crimes in a deep religious fervor. As one of them wrote, socialism was their faith; the people—its god. "Under existing conditions," one of the terrorist leaflets declared, "political murder is the only means of self-defense and one of the most effective methods of propaganda." A number of high officials of the regime were assassinated, among them the military governor of St. Petersburg in 1878 whose assailant Vera Zasulich (1849-1919) was acquitted in a famous trial. Several daring attempts were made upon the life of the tsar.

In 1879 *Zemlya i volya* split. One group under the leadership of Sophia Perovsky (1853-1881), the daughter of a former Governor-General of St. Petersburg, stressed the *Volya* aspect of the program and called itself *Na-rodnaya volya* (People's Freedom). The other group, called *Cherny peredel* (Black [or illegal, total] redistribution of the land), wished to continue the *Zemlya* program without violence. It was the former group which developed the terrorist activities. It succeeded in assassinating the "Tsar-Liberator" himself on Sunday, March 13, 1881, on the very same day when Alexander II intended to sign a decree for a very limited liberalization of the regime. The decree was drafted by Count Mikhail Loris-Melikov (1825-1888) who was the son of an Armenian merchant and who had distinguished himself as a general in the war against Turkey in 1878. Appointed chief of the Supreme Executive Commission which was to deal with revolutionary agitation, he recommended administrative and economic reforms to win over part of the moderate opposition; the decree embodied some of his proposals in a very much-watered-down form. But even these were never put into force. The successor to the Russian throne, Alexander III, adopted a strongly reactionary policy and Count Loris-Melikov immediately retired, his attempts at a moderate reform having failed as completely as those planned under Alexander I. (*See Readings Nos. 12 and 13.*)

7. **The Foreign Policy of Alexander II.** After the defeat in the Crimean War, which was felt as a deep humiliation, Alexander II tried to reestablish Russia's prestige as a great power. Therein he was supported by a growing wave of aggressive nationalism among the

Russians. In the Near East, in Central Asia, and in the Far East, his military ventures were crowned with success. Yet, as Mikhail Florinsky pointed out, these successes hardly corresponded with Russia's true interests. "A country already over-sized and under-populated, hopelessly backward industrially and culturally, squandered her scant resources of men and treasure in conquests of the arid wastes of Asia and in unrewarding adventures in the Balkans. The expansion of the imperial frontier traced on the map in blood and iron flattered, no doubt, national *amour propre;* this superficial and unreasoned satisfaction, however, was purchased at the exorbitant cost of retarding Russia's political, social, and economic progress. An aggressive foreign policy, even if successful, contains a seed of future conflicts."

In the 1860's Russia attacked the three Mohammedan principalities of Kokand, Bukhara, and Khiva in Central Asia and easily defeated their primitive armies. The important cities of Tashkent and Samarkand became centers of Russian colonial activities. The Russian general Mikhail Skobelev (1843-1882) gained wide fame by his conquests of Turkmenistan east of the Caspian Sea. The trade routes to Persia and Afghanistan and thereby to India thus came under Russian control. The Russian advance through Central Asia increased British fears of a coming conflict with Russia over Asia. Russia imposed on the conquered territories a harsh rule that led to many native revolts which in turn were cruelly suppressed. A famous Hungarian Orientalist and explorer Arminius Vambéry, in his important study *Western Culture in Eastern Lands,* compared the methods adopted by England and Russia in their Asian possessions and arrived at an unfavorable conclusion regarding the condition of the natives in the Russian colonies.

Of even greater importance was the Russian acquisition of the Chinese territory north of the Amur River and of the area between the Ussuri River and the Sea of Japan. In the latter, the Russians built the city and port of Vladivostok (1860), the name of which significantly meant "Ruler of the East." The later aggressive Russian foreign policy directed against Manchuria, Korea, and Japan had its beginning in this acquisition which was followed in 1875 by that of the large and important

island of Sakhalin from Japan in exchange for the Kurile
Islands which were occupied by the Russians in the
eighteenth century. On the other hand, the Russian government found the Russian-American Company, established in 1799 for the settlement and exploitation of
Alaska and the North American coast down to the 55th
parallel, a financial and economic failure. In her opposition to Britain, Russia was willing to sell Alaska to the
United States and, by the treaty of March 29, 1867, all
the properties of the Russian-American Company were
acquired by the United States for a sum of $7,200,000.
The transaction was at the time popular neither in Russia nor in the United States.

In spite of Russia's vast expansion in Asia, her attention during the reign of Alexander II remained concentrated on Europe and its foreign affairs. There Russian
foreign policy, directed by Prince Alexander Gorchakov
(1798-1883), was less successful. He was not equal to
the great statesmen of the period, Bismarck and Disraeli.
A descendant of an old Russian noble family, and himself highly educated and well-conversant with the West,
he was appointed in 1856 successor to Count Karl Nes-
selrode (1780-1862), who was a typical nobleman of
German origin, a member of the Church of England,
and representative of the nobilitarian and cosmopolitan
diplomacy of the period of the Holy Alliance. Nessel-
rode had been Russian foreign secretary for forty years.
Compared with him, Gorchakov represented a much
more nationalist trend in foreign policy and gained wide
popularity in Russia by the strong stand he took in 1863
against European intervention in favor of the Polish
insurgents. He cordially backed Prussia in her wars
against Denmark, Austria, and France. It was this Russian backing which made Bismarck's triumphant diplomacy against Francis Joseph and Napoleon III possible. On the other hand, Bismarck's support allowed
Russia in 1871 to denounce the clauses of the Treaty
of Paris (1856) which had imposed upon her the neutralization of the Black Sea. In 1873 the emperors of
Russia, Austria, and Germany signed a convention for
the common support of their conservative policies, but
Russian nationalist circles looked with disfavor on the
growing strength of the new German Empire created by

Prussia under Bismarck's leadership; at the same time
Bismarck became increasingly convinced that he no
longer needed Russia's support. This situation led to a
lasting estrangement between Bismarck and Gorchakov
after 1875, and finally brought about Russia's rapprochement with France.

8. Pan Slavism. The Pan Slav movement grew
out of the Slavophil movement, but whereas the latter
was spiritual and religious, Pan Slavism was political.
Slavophilism stressed the fundamental difference between the Western Germano-Latin civilization and the
Byzantine-Russian civilization, proclaimed to be different not only in degree but in substance—the latter being
much superior to the former. Pan Slavism added the
belief in the inevitable conflict between the two worlds
of Europe and Russia, out of which Russia and the
Slavs would emerge victorious. The Pan Slav theory was
systematically developed by Nicolai Danilevsky (1822-
1885) in his book *Russia and Europe, an Inquiry into
the Cultural and Political Relations of the Slav World
and of the Germano-Latin World* (1869). The book was
enthusiastically acclaimed by Dostoevsky.

Danilevsky rejected the view that modern Western
civilization was final and universally valid. A new historical civilization, that of the Slavic Russians, was now
emerging. By the necessity of historical laws it would
become the heir and successor to decaying Western civilization. Therefore, Danilevsky believed, the West necessarily felt an instinctive hostility toward its "heir and
successor." Western civilization was dominated by the
spirit of violence and capitalistic greed, whereas Slav-
Russian civilization proceeded by peaceful ways, guided
by the ideal of social justice. Russia was too great to
be only one of the powers of Europe. She was a leading
world power and had to realize her unique destiny. To
that end she had to unite all of Europe east of a line
running from Stettin on the Baltic Sea to the eastern
shores of the Adriatic Sea under her leadership. Thus
Danilevsky argued in 1869. His geographic dream was
fulfilled only by Stalin in 1945 and then for only a brief
time until the nationalism of the subject Slav peoples—
Yugoslavs and Poles—asserted itself. Like the communists, Danilevsky maintained that the expansion of West-

ern nations and Russian expansion had nothing in common: Western imperialism enslaved peoples and numbed
their growth, whereas Russian expansion liberated them.
Like a modern Russian Marxist, Danilevsky was absolutely convinced that history was on Russia's side: "It
is as impossible to fight the historical cause of events
as it is impossible to fight superior force," he wrote.
"From these general considerations we gain the certitude
that the Russian and Slav sacred cause, which is in truth
the universal and pan-human cause, cannot fail." (*See
Reading No. 14.*)

Russian Pan Slavism was not only rejected by the
Russian liberals but also by the other Slav peoples. "The
mistake of the Slavophils," Herzen wrote in *My Past
and Thoughts,* "lies in their imagining that Russia once
had an individual culture, obscured by various events
and finally by the Petersburg period. Russia never had
this culture, never could have had it. . . . Only the
mighty thought of the West to which all its long history
has led is able to fertilize the seeds slumbering in the
patriarchal mode of life of the Slavs." The non-Russian
Slavs insisted upon their own nationalism and national
cultures as opposed to Russian Pan Slav desires to impose the Russian way on them. The two most numerous
Slav peoples besides the Russians—the Ukrainians and
the Poles—lived under Russian domination and felt more
oppressed than the Slavs outside the Russian empire.
Culturally, the western Slavs looked to France and Germany and not to Russia. Nevertheless the Russian Pan
Slavs claimed that Russia had a sacred mission of lib-
erating the Slavs in the Austro-Hungarian and the Turkish empires.

Pan Slavism played a major role in Russian foreign
policy only briefly in the 1870's, and this was due to
Count Nicolai Ignatiev (1832-1908), a fervent Pan Slav-
ist, who was Russian ambassador in Constantinople from
1864 to 1877. Russian control of Constantinople—the
old imperial city of the Eastern emperors—and of the
strategically important Straits was one of the main
points of the Pan Slav program. Ignatiev intrigued to
bring the Christian nationalities in the Turkish empire,
especially the Bulgarians, under Russian influence. He
was mainly instrumental in bringing about the Russian-

Turkish War of 1877. During this war Pan Slavism, especially in Dostoevsky's writings, was used to arouse Russian nationalist mass emotion.

9. **The Balkan War.** In 1875 the Slav-speaking Turkish subjects in Bulgaria and Bosnia-Herzegovina rose against the Turks who in turn subjected the insurgents to savage reprisals. To help them, the independent Slav Balkan principalities of Serbia and Montenegro declared war on Turkey but were defeated. Russian volunteers who had fought on the side of the Serbs were killed. Russia suggested a joint intervention by the European powers, but England and Austria showed no eagerness to participate in such a step. Britain under Disraeli was deeply concerned with keeping Russia out of Turkey and the eastern Mediterranean, which had just then gained additional strategic importance by the opening of the Suez Canal (1869). Austria, eliminated from her former influence in Germany and Italy by the war of 1866, looked to the Balkans for compensation and thus was eager to keep Russia from gaining control there. Under the circumstances, Russia was willing to go it alone.

In June, 1877, the Russian armies, supported by the new principality of Rumania which was formed in 1859 from the union of Moldavia and Wallachia, crossed the Danube into the Balkan peninsula. The Turks defended Plevna and the Shipka Pass in the Balkan Mountains for several months, but in January the Russians occupied Bulgaria's two most important cities, Sofia and Philippopolis, marched to Adrianople, and reached the Sea of Marmora. Facing defeat, the Turks sued for peace. A treaty signed at San Stefano on the Sea of Marmora in February, 1878, not only reduced the Turkish territory in Europe to a considerable extent but also created a great Bulgaria including most of Macedonia. The Russians expected that, being the liberator of Bulgaria, they would acquire predominant influence over the new nation. Britain and Austria objected to such Russian aggrandizement. The "war of nerves" skillfully managed by Disraeli induced Russia to abandon the Treaty of San Stefano and to agree upon an international congress to settle the fate of the Balkans.

10. **The Congress of Berlin.** This congress met in

Berlin in June, 1878, under the chairmanship of the
German Chancellor Prince Bismarck. There Disraeli succeeded in fulfilling his aims. Bulgaria was greatly reduced
in size; Bosnia and Herzegovina officially continued to
be a part of Turkey but were placed under Austrian
administration; Turkey remained a power in Europe.
Russia received only southwestern Bessarabia and the
cities of Kars, Ardahan, and Batum in Asiatic Turkey.
To enable Britain to protect Asiatic Turkey against further Russian encroachments, Turkey ceded the administration of the Turkish island of Cyprus to Britain. England thereby strengthened her strategic position in the
eastern Mediterranean; this step became of even greater
importance when four years later Britain occupied the
Turkish autonomous province of Egypt and its Suez
Canal.

The Congress of Berlin had far-reaching consequences.
It marked a diplomatic defeat for Russia who saw herself deprived of the fruit of her victory over Turkey.
For the following decades the Balkans remained the
cockpit of European diplomacy. Russian, Austrian, and
British interests conflicted there. Austria felt herself
threatened by Pan Slav and Yugoslav plans directed at
her dismemberment, and trusted for her preservation in
German support. In October, 1879, Germany and Austria concluded the Dual Alliance, which by Italy's accession three years later was enlarged into the Triple
Alliance. The Austro-German alliance was directed predominantly against Russia. Since the time of the Napoleonic wars, Russia had relied, above all, upon cooperation with Prussia. Now the Russians, feeling let
down by the Germans, went through a fundamental and
painful reappraisal of their traditional foreign policy.
Like France, Russia believed herself threatened by Germany's ill-defined aggressive policy. Thus it came about
that Russia, the pillar of autocracy in Europe, was ready,
despite deep ideological differences, to turn to France
where in those years the Third Republic claimed to represent the traditions of the French Revolution. The common fear of a Germany which was steadily growing
more powerful overcame the ideological distrust between
autocracy and democracy. In that way the Berlin Congress planted the seed not only of the Balkan wars of

1912-13 but also of the First World War which broke
out as the result of the acute tensions between an Austria backed by Germany and a Serbia which was supported by Russia and had been victorious over Turkey.
Fearing that such a conflict would end in an Austro-
German victory over Russia which would isolate France
on the European continent, France came to Russia's
support and thus the Balkan conflict widened into the
Great European War. This event, however, was still far
in the future when Alexander III ascended the Russian
imperial throne.

— 5 —

THE REASSERTION OF AUTOCRACY

1. Alexander III. The new emperor was determined to avenge the death of his father and to put an
end to all revolutionary activities. His former tutor Constantine Pobyedonostsev (1827-1907), who had been
professor of Russian law at the University of Moscow,
exercised great influence over him. A man of scholarly
training, Pobyedonostsev was a firm believer in the un-
surpassed virtues of autocracy and in the necessity of
strengthening the Orthodox Church and Russian nationalism as the unshakable bulwarks of the Russian empire.
He had no doubt about the moral and practical evil of
all modern Western institutions and their total inappli-
cability to Russia. As decisively as the Russian communists did later, Pobyedonostsev rejected parliamentary
democracy, freedom of the press, independence of the
judiciary, and declared himself at the same time a
staunch champion of the common people. In his *Reflections of a Russian Statesman* (*see Reading No. 15*)

he maintained that in the Western democracies the real rulers were the dexterous manipulators of votes, that the so-called free elections in no way expressed the will of the voters, and that the people in Western countries groaned under the despotism of parliamentarism and recognized its faults. The official position which Pobyedonostsev held from 1880 to 1905 was that of the chief procurator or chairman of the Holy Synod. During that period he was regarded as the most influential single man in Russia.

Under his influence the feeble trends toward legality in Russia which had developed during the earlier part of the reign of Alexander II were not only abandoned but reversed. A statute of August, 1881, enacted originally only as a temporary measure for three years, empowered the government to proclaim a state of emergency wherever needed, and under this regime officials could arrest and fine without a trial, re-assign cases from civilian to military courts, close schools, and suspend periodicals. This "temporary" police regime remained in force until March, 1917, when the democratic revolution abolished it completely, though only for the short period of its own brief duration. The very restricted local self-government introduced under Alexander II was curtailed under Alexander III and the nobility was given a preponderant influence in whatever remained. Further, though the framework created by the reforms of the 1860's was maintained, its "liberal" contents, not too substantial even at the beginning, were decimated. The same fate befell the educational reforms. The autonomy of the universities was abolished; professors and students alike were closely supervised; higher education was to be limited to "reliable" elements of the population and had to be conducted on strictly official and orthodox lines. The foundations of moderate progress and lawful development, for which the educated Russian classes had strived in the 1860's, were fatally weakened in the 1880's. (*See Reading No. 16.*)

2. The Russification Policy. Pobyedonostsev wished to make the closely integrated twin forces of Russian nationalism and the Orthodox Church the only legally admitted institutions of cultural and spiritual life in the Russian empire, notwithstanding the fact that more than

half the population was non-Russian, and that there were
substantial numbers professing the Mohammedan, Roman Catholic, Jewish, or Protestant faith. The use of the
Ukrainian, Byelorussian, and Lithuanian languages was
forbidden, and no books could be published in them.
All instruction in Poland and in the Baltic provinces
was to be given in Russian and no longer in Polish or
German. The Roman Catholic and the Protestant
Churches were treated without tolerance. Conversion to
the Orthodox faith was promoted by all possible means.
The Russian empire was to be, as far as possible, a
monolithic bloc with one ruler, one faith, one law, and
one language. Only in Finland were the local rights respected. Not until the 1890's did the wave of Russification reach Finland, where the population, educated
through its long connection with Sweden in the Scandinavian tradition, resisted resolutely.

The hardest hit inhabitants of the Russian empire were
the Jews. Anti-Semitism became one of the salient fea-
tures of Pobyedonostsev's regime. The administration
itself helped to undermine the foundations of law by
unchaining the xenophobic religious bigotry of the masses
and by conniving to permit the excesses of the hooligans
in murdering Jews and pillaging their property. That this
lawlessness, promoted by the government, could one day
turn against the landowners and even against itself was
overlooked by the government. Education toward legal
responsibility among the people was outside the scope
of an autocratic regime. A wave of pogroms—the word
meaning "devastation" in Russian—swept Russia in 1881,
especially in the southwest. The massacres of the Jews
aroused widespread protests in Western countries, above
all in Britain. In Russia these pogroms marked the beginning of the mass emigration of Russian Jews to Western Europe and even more to the United States.

The pogroms lasted until April, 1882, when the government introduced extraordinary legislation to prevent
the "exploitation" of the true Russian people by the
Jews. The Jews were allowed to live only in the western
and southwestern provinces of the empire, and there
only in the towns and not in the rural areas. They were
not allowed to acquire any agrarian property. In 1887 a
numerus clausus (quota system) for the admission of

Jewish students to high schools and colleges was introduced. Their number was limited to three percent in
Moscow and St. Petersburg and to ten percent in the
Jewish pale, the region in which Jews were compelled to
live. Wherever possible, they were forced out of the pro-
fessions and all enterprises of a semi-official character.
In 1889 the legal career was closed to them. Special
taxes were imposed upon them and a law of 1893 made
the use of Christian names by Jews a criminal offense.
In addition to this "legal" anti-Semitism, the Jews were
subjected to innumerable arbitrary humiliations and depredations by local authorities.

It should be pointed out, however, that Russian anti-
Semitism had no racial basis as did Hitler's. A Jew who
accepted the Orthodox faith enjoyed all the rights and
privileges of other members of the Church. Moreover,
a committee of high officials appointed by the government opposed discrimination against Jews and insisted
that there was only one way and one solution to the
Jewish problem—"the emancipation of the Jews and
their assimilation with the rest of the population under
the protection of the same laws." The opinion given by
these conservative officials reflected widespread opposition even among the nobility and the higher bureaucracy
against the extreme reactionary course pursued by the
autocracy. But nothing swayed Alexander III and
Pobyedonostsev from the position which they regarded
as the only one capable of guaranteeing the salvation
of Russia. And for the time being they seemed to be
right. The revolutionary movement was successfully suppressed and Russia seemed to be stable, quiet, and strong
as she had been under Nicolai I. The tsar's relatively short
reign came to an end after only thirteen years. It was the
only reign in modern Russian history in which the
country was not waging a major war. Alexander III
died in 1894 and was succeeded by his son Nicolai II
who was determined to continue the policy of his father
and to be guided by the political philosophy and advice of
Pobyedonostsev.

3. Economic Development. The antiquated and
semi-Oriental autocracy of Alexander III was in sharp
contrast to the economic development of that period.
Modern capitalist and industrial economy was brought

to Russia, largely in order to make the modernization of the military establishment possible. But this technologically advanced economy had to be superimposed on a backward agrarian economy and its communal organization. Whereas in Germany the harvest of an acre of wheat amounted to 1,109 pounds, in Russia it amounted to only 406 pounds. The agrarian productivity was too low to feed the rapidly growing number of peasants; yet more than three-fourths of the population was engaged in agriculture. But in relative figures, the industrialization of Russia progressed considerably. As Professor Warren B. Walsh pointed out, the value of the aggregate industrial output of Russia increased from 541 millions of rubles in 1871 to nearly 6,000 millions in 1912, the production of pig iron rose from 1.3 millions of tons in 1894 to 5.1 million in 1913, and the mining of coal from 18,000 tons in 1900 to 40 million tons in 1913. Great progress was also made in the building of railroads, and the first steps were taken in the 1880's to introduce modern labor legislation. But many of these factory laws were not enforced, and the condition of the workers remained miserable.

One of the most important personalities in the industrialization of Russia was Count Sergei Witte (1849-1915), a specialist in railway transportation. In 1892 he became minister of ways of communication and, in the following year, minister of finance. He was an ardent disciple of the nationalist system of economy proposed half a century before by the German Friedrich List. Except in the field of economic modernization, Witte himself was a reactionary and an adherent of autocracy. He believed that a centralized dictatorial control would permit the development of a truly planned progressive economy and thus would prove much superior to a democratic regime where conflicts of parliamentary parties and pressure groups made any large-scale planning impossible. But the remarkable outward improvement of Russian economy was accompanied by many glaring defects. The policy of forced exportation of wheat and other agricultural products and the imposition of high tariffs for the importation of manufactured goods contributed to a rapid impoverishment of the peasants. Their situation was worsened by repeated famines of which that of 1891 had effects as devastating as those after the communist revolution. The burden of taxation fell heaviest on the peasantry. Whereas the nobility could receive loans on easy terms, the peasants had to pay a very high rate of interest, much more than they could economically afford. In spite of the preference shown the nobility, not only peasant agriculture decayed but also that of the nobility. On the other hand, the state finances no longer faced the former deficits; the governmental gold reserves grew, thanks to a favorable trade balance; and in 1896, Witte could stabilize the ruble on a gold basis. Under these conditions he was able to attract many foreign investments, especially French and Belgian, in Russian industry and railroad building. The Russian government too borrowed money abroad. The public debt owed abroad increased from 1.733 million rubles in 1894 to 4,299 million rubles in 1914. Of this debt, about four-fifths was owed to France. French investors were attracted by political reasons; the money was to strengthen the military power of Russia as France's only ally.

Russian industrialization under Witte was top-heavy as it continued to be later under Stalin. Heavy industry was favored by the government in every way, but light industry lagged behind and consumer goods were therefore very expensive and inaccessible to the masses. The government played a great role in much of the spectacular industrialization of the country, whereas the *zemstvos* encouraged the growth of household industries in the villages and the formation of cooperative groups of artisans called *artels*. All these developments helped to create for the first time an active middle class and especially an industrial proletariat in Russia. Driven by their misery, many peasants migrated to the cities and thus provided a supply of cheap labor. As it was illegal to organize trade unions to voice the dissatisfaction and demands of the new proletariat, they easily became the backbone of revolutionary movements. In the 1890's the first organized mass strikes took place, not for political demands but for the amelioration of the wretched working conditions. These circumstances transformed the Russian revolutionary movement, which shifted its emphasis from the peasants to the industrial workers.

4. The Russian Revolutionary Movement. The energetic measures taken by the government after 1881 succeeded in at least temporarily crushing the terrorist movement. An isolated plot against the life of Alexander III in 1887 was remarkable only by the fact that one of the young men involved and executed was Lenin's older brother Alexander. Most of the leaders of the terrorist movement were either in prison or abroad. The populism of the 1870's which had started with such high idealistic hopes and declamations apparently ended in failure: the terrorist actions had not moved the government toward constitutional reforms but had increased the trend toward reaction; the peasantry had not been aroused but remained completely irresponsive. Thus the late 1880's marked the beginning of a new phase of the revolutionary movement; it no longer relied on a peculiar brand of Russian socialism but accepted the "scientific" socialism propagated in Western Europe by Karl Marx, who died in 1883, and by his friend Friedrich Engels, who was to survive Marx until 1892. As early as 1862 their famous *Communist Manifesto* had appeared in Russian, translated by Bakunin and printed in London by Herzen. Ten years later the first volume of *Das Kapital* was brought out in a Russian translation in St. Petersburg, and though it was immediately banned by the censors, it could claim the distinction of being the first translation of the famous work into any foreign language—the first English edition appeared only in 1887.

The first Russian Marxist theoretician, the father of Russian Marxism, was George Plekhanov (1857-1918), who in 1883 founded in Geneva a group called *Osvobozhdenie Truda* (Liberation of Labor). Plekhanov and his friend Paul Axelrod (1850-1928) believed that Russia would follow the general trend of Western Europe and would have to pass through the stage of capitalism and middle-class revolution before arriving at socialism. They rejected the populist view that the Russian village commune afforded protection against the spread of capitalism, and contended that capitalism was entering the villages through the development of a class of rich peasants, or *kulaks*. They accepted Marx's theory that Russia, being backward as a capitalistic country, was further removed from socialism than the advanced Western countries.

The growth of capitalism would put an end to Russian autocracy and usher in a democratic regime. Russian social democracy, Plekhanov taught, should not prematurely provoke a revolution in Russia but should educate the Russian proletariat to follow the lead of the Western workers so that they would be prepared whenever the latter assumed power in their countries. Thus Plekhanov's theory was a complete negation of the Russian nationalist and romantic agrarian socialism of the populists. But the influence of Marxism did not grow in Russia, nor was the revolutionary movement revived before the beginning of the twentieth century. By then, Nicolai II had succeeded his father to the throne after the latter's death in 1894.

5. **Nicolai II.** On his deathbed, Alexander III adjured his son to maintain steadfastly the principle of autocracy. Alexander's widow admonished Nicolai II to accept Pobyedonostsev's advice in all matters. The new emperor, a man of simple mind and manners, remained all his life convinced of the superiority and necessity of autocracy for Russia, but he himself had neither the will power nor the strength of character of a true autocrat. He easily succumbed to the influences of stronger, though not wiser personalities—first of his mother, then of his wife, a German princess who was a granddaughter of Queen Victoria of England and who had spent much of her youth at the English court. The emperor and empress, who had an unusually happy marriage and were devoted to each other, conversed and corresponded mostly in English, but in spite of her upbringing in England, the empress was hostile to all constitutional ideas. She was most eager to preserve the full integrity of autocratic power for her husband, whom she regarded as a stronger and more capable man than he really was, and later, after the arrival of the long-awaited heir to the throne, for her son.

Public opinion in Russia first greeted the new emperor in the hope that with him a new liberal era would dawn. These expectations were quickly dashed when Nicolai assured the *zemstvo* delegates, to their consternation, that he would safeguard the principle of autocracy as firmly and unyieldingly as did his father. He characterized as a senseless dream the idea then widely held in Russian society that representatives of the *zemstvos* might participate in the administration of national affairs. Nicolai II stubbornly clung to all the old advisers and methods of his father. But in his weaker hands they revealed themselves to be instruments entirely incapable of coping with the growing social and intellectual unrest in the country.

This unrest was stimulated by the general economic progress. Witte was building a railroad crossing the immense span of Siberia from the Ural Mountains to the Pacific Ocean, thus opening up the Siberian lands to settlement. In the Caucasus, Russia produced half of the world's petroleum; from the oilfields at Baku on the Caspian Sea, a pipeline was built to Batum on the Black Sea. Russian central Asia was traversed by a railroad from the Caspian Sea to the border of China and another railroad connected Tashkent, the largest city of Russian central Asia, with European Russia across the steppes of Orenburg. Great strikes in 1896 were followed a year later by legislation which granted factory labor an 11½-hour work-day with 10 hours on Saturday, prohibited work on Sunday and seventeen holidays, and restricted overtime to 120 hours a year. But Russia was no nearer to representative government in 1900 than she had been in 1825 when the Decembrists demanded a constitution. There were no legal institutions to provide a forum for voicing demands for reform. Thus all political activity was driven into illegal channels. (*See Reading No. 17.*)

6. **The Russian Revolutionary Movement Continues.** In 1895 Plekhanov's disciples began to carry Marxist propaganda into factories and workshops. Under the leadership of Lenin and Julius Martov (1873-1923), a Fighting Union for the Liberation of the Working Class was organized in St. Petersburg—the name being indicative of the greater emphasis on struggle and class. Lenin (1870-1924), whose original name was Vladimir Ulyanov, was born in Simbirsk, a city on the Volga River today called Ulyanovsk. He was the son of a government official, the inspector of the schools in the Simbirsk region. As a student, Lenin was expelled from his university for revolutionary activities and then dedicated himself to the study of Marxist literature. In contrast to Plekhanov, Lenin regarded the peasantry, as Ba-

kunin had before him, as a potentially revolutionary element and expected the Russian revolution to come much
sooner than did the father of Russian Marxism. In 1897
Lenin was exiled to Siberia where, like other political
prisoners, he had the opportunity of studying and writing.
In 1899 he could even legally publish his first major
work, *The Development of Capitalism in Russia,* a book
of more than 600 pages. In 1900 he was allowed to
return to European Russia. In order to publish his works
free from censorship, he left Russia in the summer of
1900 and went to Geneva where he met Plekhanov and
became one of the editors of the newspaper *Iskra* (*The
Spark*). Its name was derived from a line in a Decembrist
poem—"From the spark the flame will burst forth."
From the very beginning of his writings Lenin directed
a relentless and ruthless polemic against all socialists
who disagreed with him in the slightest. He insisted that
the working class must never submit to any compromise; that there could be nothing in common between
the socialists of his kind and any moderate group; above
all, that the Russian workers need not postpone their
revolution until capitalism in Russia had matured. Russia was the weakest link in the chain of European capitalism; for that very reason, Lenin maintained, the
social revolution would start in Russia. Therefore it is not
astonishing that Lenin, who continued the tradition of
Russian extremist sectarianism, brought about a split in
the Russian (Marxist) Social Democratic Party.

This party had been founded at a congress held at
Minsk in western Russia in 1898. The party was still insignificant in numbers, but it counted in its ranks some
gifted young economists and scholars such as Mikhail
Tugan-Baranovsky (1865-1919), Peter Struve (1870-
1944), and Sergei Bulgakov (1871-1944). The factional
dissensions among the Russian Marxists came to a head
at the second party congress which was held in 1903 in
Brussels and transferred from there to London. The faction led by Lenin and called *Bolshevik,* which in Russian
means majority group, was at the same time the maxi-
malist group. The minority group, or in Russian, *Mensheviks,* was willing to accept a democratic republic as a
stage on the road to socialism, and therefore to cooperate with liberal elements. On the other hand, the Bolshe-

viks demanded the immediate creation of the dictatorship of the proletariat, which would treat the bourgeoisie
as an implacable enemy. The Mensheviks, who stood for
Marxists principles as generally understood in the West,
favored a large democratic mass party of the workers as
it existed in Germany; the Bolsheviks, guided by the Russian tradition of revolutionary conspiracy, insisted on a
small and select party consisting of determined revolutionaries under a strictly centralized authoritarian leadership so that the group, though representing only a small
minority of the people, could seize power by disciplined
and resolute action when the opportune moment arrived.

The Marxists of radical and moderate complexion,
however, were not the only organized Russian revolutionaries at the beginning of the twentieth century. The
populist movement with its emphasis on the peasantry
and on individual heroism was revived in 1900 when the
Russian Socialist Revolutionary Party, generally known
as S.R., was founded. In many ways this party was nearer
to the Mensheviks, but it differed from them in its
acceptance of political terror. After 1902 a number of
terrorist attempts to assassinate leading personalities of
the tsarist regime were organized by the Fighting Organization (*Boyevaya Organizatsiya*) of the Socialist Revolutionaries. Most of the terrorists were dedicated idealists,
young men and women who came from all classes including high officialdom and the aristocracy. But the
unavoidable secrecy surrounding all their activities and
the similarly cunning counter-actions of the secret police
led to suspicions and temptations of all kinds. Thus it
was proven in 1908 that the supreme head of the terrorist organization, Erno Azef, who had successfully
plotted several sensational assassinations, was at the same
time in the pay of the secret police. This in no way isolated fact—later on it was revealed that Roman Malinov-
sky, the leader of the Bolshevik Party in the Russian
duma in the years before World War I, was a police agent
and that his violent anti-government speeches were submitted to and approved by the police—temporarily discredited terrorism. One of its leaders, Boris Savinkov
(1879-1925) in 1905 organized the assassination of
Grand Duke Sergei. He was condemned to death but
escaped to Switzerland and wrote two novels, *The Pale*

Horse (1909) and *That Which Never Happened* (1913)
—which give a most interesting dissection of a terrorist's
mind. In 1917, like so many other revolutionaries, he
returned to Russia where he strongly opposed the Bolsheviks. The best known among the other Social Revolutionary leaders were Victor Chernov (1876-1952), one
of the party theoreticians, and Catherine Breshko-Bresh-
kovskaya (1844-1934). Her life was typical of many
other Russian revolutionaries. Born of a wealthy and
noble family, she left her home as a young woman to
spread revolutionary doctrines among the peasants. She
was imprisoned for twenty-two years in St. Petersburg
and Siberia, much of the time in close confinement. After
having participated in the Russian revolution of 1905
she was again imprisoned and banished to Siberia, but
was released in 1917, a woman in her seventies, widely
known and venerated throughout Russia as the "Grand-
mother of the Russian Revolution." After Lenin's seizure
of power she was again forced into exile and died abroad
in her ninetieth year.

7. **The Birth of a Liberal Movement.** The 1890's
also witnessed in Russia the birth of a liberal movement
inspired by Western constitutional ideas. At that time
some of the leaders of the *zemstvos,* men of undoubted
patriotism and loyalty, started to organize societies for
the advancement of literacy, for the improvement of
health, and other desirable and long over-due reforms.
But the government, instead of welcoming these attempts,
persecuted their initiators and dissolved the societies.
Thus hindered in all legal activity, some liberal leaders
decided in 1902 to publish abroad a periodical called
Osvobozhdeniye (*Liberation*), edited by the former
Marxist Peter Struve. In 1903 they founded the Union of
Liberation, among whose members were prominent
liberal aristocrats such as Prince Lvov, scholars such as
the historian Pavel Milyukov (1859-1943) and the jurist
Sergei Muromtsev (1850-1910), and writers such as the
novelist Vladimir Korolenko (1853-1921). Out of this
Union in 1905 emerged the Constitutional Democratic
Party, whose members were generally known as "Kadets," an abbreviation formed by the initials of the Russian name of the party. Consisting of highly educated
and patriotic citizens, the liberal party could have grown

into the instrument for transforming Russian autocracy into a regime of liberty under law. Three reasons prevented such a development: the conceited stubbornness and the malevolent stupidity of the government; the lack of parliamentary experience in Russia; and the chaos which the First World War, coming a decade after the formation of the Constitutional Democratic Party, produced. Many precious and promising seeds of a free Russia and a full partner of the European community were sown during the course of modern Russian history, but human failure and historical contingency did not grant them time to ripen.

8. Mounting Reaction. Faced by the growing unrest in the country, the government showed itself at first not only unwilling to make any substantial concessions to the demands for liberty and social reform but insisted upon intensifying the unyielding character of its autocracy. The ministers appointed by Nicolai II were mostly old-style mediocre bureaucrats without vision. More energetic was Vyacheslav Plehve (1846-1904), appointed in 1902 to the key position of Minister of the Interior. But his energies were put into the service of reactionary repression. He carried on with redoubled zeal the Russification of the non-Russian parts of the empire, especially of Finland. He opposed Witte's policy for the modernization of the Russian economy because it would create a prosperous middle class which could become a factor dangerous to the continuation of the autocracy. Under his administration a new wave of pogroms similar to those of 1881 swept southwestern Russia. The most important among them was the massacre of the Jews in Kishenev, Bessarabia, on Easter Day, 1903. These pogroms not only aroused deep indignation abroad; together with Plehve's extreme Russification policy for the minorities, they made him the most hated symbol of the regime. Thus it is understandable that he fell victim to a terrorist act in July, 1904. The assassination came at a time when Russia, in spite of its domestic tensions and backwardness, was involved in a major war against Japan, a war provoked by Russia's rapacious imperialism.

In Europe, the first decade of Nicolai II's regime saw the strengthening of the Russian alliance with France. At the same time, while avoiding military adventures in

Europe, Russian foreign policy concentrated on the Far
East. Weakened at home by economic backwardness and
threatened with internal strife, the regime, instead of
undertaking domestic reforms, thought of finding a way
out by gaining easy successes abroad and thus restoring
its waning prestige. Yet the same Russian government
which was bent on military ventures posed simultaneously
as a fervent supporter of universal peace and as the initia-
tor of a movement for universal reduction of armaments.
In 1898 the tsar's government proposed an international
conference to that end. The conference met in 1899 at
The Hague, and was followed by a second, again called
on Russian initiative in 1907. The conferences, the call-
ing of which would be characterized today as propaganda
moves, ended without any real achievements. Only seven
years after the second conference closed, the greatest war
up to that time started, and Russia had played a major
and perhaps decisive role in originating World War I.
But even while the first conference at The Hague was in
session, Russian troops were busy creating the conditions
that made the war with Japan five years later inevitable.

   9. Russia's Far Eastern Policy.   As Crown Prince,
Nicolai II had visited the Far East in 1891. From that
moment on, Russian official attention was riveted on
grandiose and ambitious goals in China and Japan. The
dream of assuming the imperial succession of Byzantium
through the control of Constantinople and the Near East
had faded for the time being after the diplomatic defeat
of 1878. Another imperial dream, the succession to the
great Mongol emperors whose hold on Russia had been
broken in the sixteenth century, was revived instead.
Crown Prince Nicolai's companion on the Far East
voyage wrote that the time had come that the Russians
should acknowledge the inheritance left them by Ghengis
Khan and should put themselves at the head of the under-
developed peoples of the Orient. The more realistic Witte
believed in expansion in Asia too: he saw the trans-Siberian railroad, which he had built as a means of intensifying Russian Far Eastern trade and of even supplanting
the Suez Canal, as the great trade route to the Orient.
An alliance between Russia and China in which, of
course, Russia would be the dominant partner appeared

the best means of undermining or overthrowing British
political, economic, and cultural influence in Asia.

But Britain was not the only power that Russia was
to encounter in her effort to gain control of China. A
new competitor for leadership in the Far East had arisen
in Japan. Though originally infinitely more backward
than Russia, the small country of Japan, without any important economic resources, had launched in the 1860's
and 1870's a policy of economic and social modernization and liberalization of its antiquated oriental theocracy.
In this effort Japan was far more successful than Russia
in her simultaneous efforts in a similar direction. The
Japanese ruling class showed itself enlightened and efficient in the task of building a modern nation to a degree
entirely unknown in Russia. The results were seen in
1894, the year of Nicolai II's accession to the throne,
when Japan became involved in a conflict with China
over Korea. The ensuing Sino-Japanese war ended in
Japan's quick and spectacular victory. Russian intervention on behalf of China prevented the Japanese from
reaping the full fruit of their victory. They had to renounce their acquisition of the much-coveted Liaotung
Peninsula with its strategic naval base of Port Arthur.

The greater was Japanese indignation when only four
years later the Russians themselves acquired Port Arthur
and the adjacent territory through a lease from China.
Great investments were made by the Russian government
to modernize and fortify Port Arthur and the nearby
port of Talienwan, or Dairen, called by the Russians
Dalny, one of the finest harbors on the east Asian coast.
The trans-Siberian railroad was to be extended to con-
nect the ports of the Liaotung Peninsula with Russia
and Europe. The nationalist uprising in China in 1900
against the danger of a partition of the Chinese empire
by the great powers, known as the Boxer uprising, provided the Russians with a pretext for occupying the
whole of Manchuria. After the liquidation of the Boxer
rebellion, the Russian troops refused to withdraw from
Manchuria. The danger of a war with Japan was foreseen, but Russian generals and statesmen were convinced
that the Japanese army would collapse should it dare to
resist Russian expansion, and Plehve believed that a "lit-

tle victorious war" would divert attention from Russia's domestic troubles. Thus Russia proceeded to acquire important concessions on the Yalu River, which forms the border between Korea and Manchuria, and tried to convert Korea into a Russian protectorate. Japan hoped to negotiate with Russia in order to delimit by agreement the mutual spheres of interest in Korea and Manchuria, but Russia haughtily rejected all Japanese overtures.

Japan, which had entered into an alliance with Britain in 1902, was determined to resist Russian encroachments. After an ultimatum to which no reply was recevied, but without a declaration of war, the Japanese navy, on the night of February 8, 1904, attacked the Russian fleet anchored in Port Arthur and destroyed or damaged many of its units. Thus the war started. In the following spring, Japanese troops landed in northern Korea and on the Liaotung Peninsula and began a siege of Port Arthur by land. The fortified harbor was defended by the Russians as, half a century before, Sevastopol had been. But the hope that the Russian army from Manchuria, under the command of Alexei Kuropatkin (1848-1921), who had distinguished himself in the war of 1877 and had been Russian Minister of War from 1898 to 1904, would relieve Port Arthur was not realized. Port Arthur surrendered in January, 1905, and Kuropatkin was decisively defeated in the great battle of Mukden, then Manchuria's capital, strategically located for the control of all of southern Manchuria. The Russian armies were poorly equipped and badly prepared. The Japanese victory—the first major defeat of a great "white" colonial power by an Asian nation—had a resounding effect throughout Asia and was one of the chief elements in the awakening of nationalism there. This nationalism was determined to imitate the Japanese example and to prove itself equal to the "whites." In 1905 the Japanese showed themselves superior not only on land but also at sea. The Baltic Russian fleet, mighty in numbers but with antiquated armament, sailed almost 18,000 miles around Europe, Africa, and Asia to challenge the Japanese navy. But the latter, under the command of Admiral Togo, annihilated the Russian armada in the battle in the Tsushima Strait between Korea and Japan in May, 1905.

Less than three months later, peace negotiations, initiated by President Theodore Roosevelt, started in Portsmouth, New Hampshire. In the peace treaty the Russians ceded the southern half of Sakhalin Island back to Japan and recognized Japanese influence in southern Manchuria and in Korea. The Japanese also acquired extensive fishing rights of fundamental importance to their economy. Thus for the time being, Russia's dream of dominion over Asia ended in failure, to be revived only after the Bolsheviks had replaced the tsars. Of greater immediate importance, however, was the fact that the defeat in the Japanese War, like the defeat in the Crimean War, revealed the glaring inadequacies and the shocking backwardness of the proud Russian autocracry and led to a partial liberalization of the regime.

10. The Russian Revolution of 1905. The war in the Far East and the economic dislocations caused by it in Russia's large industrial centers, such as a rise in prices in no way compensated for by rising wages, led to labor unrest in St. Petersburg, and especially in the great armament factory of Putilov. Georgi Gapon (1870-1906), a young priest who played an ambiguous role as an organizer of labor in the interests of the government, led a peaceful mass demonstration of workers to the imperial palace to present the emperor with a petition signed by 135,000 persons. "We, the workers of the city of St. Petersburg," the petition began, "our wives, children, and helpless old parents, are approachng Thee, our Lord, to seek justice and protection. We live in misery, we are oppressed, we are burdened with work beyond our strength, . . . our patience is exhausted. We have arrived at the terrible situation in which death is more welcome than the continuation of our unbearable pain." Then followed a long list of demands, partly of an economic and partly of a political nature. The unarmed demonstrators, some of whom carried before them pictures of the emperor and of Orthodox saints, were met in front of the palace by troops who opened fire and killed or wounded several hundred persons.

This "Bloody Sunday" (January 22, 1905) marked the beginning of a widespread unrest and a wave of strikes. The government still was determined not to make the slightest concession. General Dmitri Trepov (1855-1906) was placed in command of St. Petersburg, and several other police officers, similarly known for their ruthlessness, were appointed to reestablish order. As a counter-measure, Grand Duke Sergei, a son of Emperor Alexander II and known as a staunch upholder of autocracy, was killed by the terrorists with a bomb. The emperor called upon "all truly Russian people" to fight the domestic enemies and promised that with God's help he would lead the Russian empire "under the banner of autocracy" out of all its difficulties to new and indestructible greatness. To counter the reformist agitation, the government organized unions of "patriots" of the extreme right. Their tough action groups, called *Cherniya Sotni* (Black Hundreds), committed innumerable atrocities against intellectuals, liberals, and minorities—especially Jews. Yet the vast majority of the peoples of the Russian empire was seized by revolutionary unrest, so that finally the autocracy, after much hesitation, found it wiser to give some ground. (*See Reading No. 18.*)

The revolutionary forces neither were organized nor did they cooperate on the basis of a clear-cut program. These forces could be roughly divided into four groups: the liberals, the peasants, the workers, and the non-Russian nationalities. On behalf of the liberals, a deputation of ten leading citizens, among them four princes, submitted a petition to the tsar in June. Their spokesman, Prince Sergei Trubetskoy (1862-1905), a professor of philosophy at the University of Moscow, implored the tsar to introduce reforms before it was too late. "Your Majesty, you hold in your hands the honor and the power of Russia and its domestic peace. Your state and your throne, inherited from your ancestors, is in your hands. Don't hesitate! In this terrible hour of the nation's trial, your responsibility before God and before Russia is great." In reply the emperor expressed the pious hope that the harmony between ruler and people would continue, as in times past, to form the foundation of an order which would correspond to the traditional principles of Russia. In this answer, the conviction held by many court circles was apparent, namely, that the tsar could rely upon the unswerving devotion of the "true people," the Russian peasants, who were supposed to be untouched by the wave of Western influences which had "corrupted" the educated class.

In that assumption the court was profoundly mistaken. Though the peasants did not raise any political demands, they suffered from severe economic grievances and were willing to appropriate by direct action the land which they believed was theirs by right. They demanded rent reduction as well as ownership of the land by those who worked it. The year 1905 saw the emergence of the first nation-wide peasant organizations, but the peasant violence strengthened a reactionary movement among some of the landowners. Thus the countryside was in the grip of violent agitation, too. Nor could the tsar rely any longer on the devotion of the armed forces. The most famous episode in that respect was the mutiny aboard the cruiser *Potyemkin* in the Black Sea on June 27. The cruiser was named after the famous chief favorite of Catherine II, Gregory Potyemkin (1739-1791), who annexed southern Russia and the Crimea to the empire and was the first to build a Russian fleet in the Black Sea. Though the mutiny lasted only one week, it exercised an influence upon the course of events. It made people think of the possibility of an armed uprising against the autocracy. The gifted Russian motion picture producer Sergei Eisenstein (1898-1948) made a famous movie of the mutiny in 1925.

More important was the revolutionary movement among the workers. A wave of strikes, of which those of typesetters and railroad workers were the most important, swept over the country. What had originally been a committee of strikers, now organized itself in St. Petersburg as a Council of Deputies of the Workers, or *soviet*—a word which means council in Russian. Similar soviets sprang up in other Russian cities, all cooperating with one another. The chairman of the St. Petersburg soviet was Leon Trotsky (1879-1940). The soviets were mostly under Menshevik influence and published an official organ called *Izvestiya* (*News*). In 1905 Bolsheviks and Mensheviks competed for the leadership of the Russian proletariat. The whole vehemence of Lenin's ruthless dogmatism revealed itself in his struggle against the Mensheviks, whom he called "agents of the bourgeoisie." Any socialist who held opinions divergent from his own was regarded as a deliberate traitor to socialism. One must understand this Leninist intolerance to comprehend the later famous Stalinist trials against "traitors" in the ranks of the socialists and communists.

No less important than the workers' movement was the widespread dissatisfaction among the many nationalities who lived in the Russian empire and were subject to a policy of sharp discrimination. Among them were peoples who possessed a long history and an old national consciousness like the Poles, Georgians, Armenians, and the Finns; others like the Mohammedan peoples of central Asia, of the lower Volga region and of the Caucasus had preserved their sense of independence and had not taken even the first steps toward an integration with the national life of Russia. A third and perhaps the most numerous group consisted of peasant peoples for whom the year 1905 marked the transition from a stage of national consciousness confined to a very small educated class to one in which the masses began to participate in the national movement. To this group belonged the Ukrainians, the Latvians, the Byelorussians, and the Lithuanians in the western provinces of the empire and some of the native peoples of Siberia and eastern Russia. Driven in the interests of their own national groups to work for a complete change in the Russian system of government, these nationalities allied themselves with the Russian revolutionary movement, though each one worked for the independence or at least the autonomy of its national group. The agitation of the year 1905 was a powerful influence in awakening the non-Russian peoples out of their lethargy. Nowhere in Europe was national repression at the beginning of the twentieth century so harsh as in Russia. Though the Russians formed only 43 percent of the population, Russian was the only official language, the only language used in government schools, in courts of justice, and in the administration.

11. A Constitutional Autocracy. Faced by the growing unrest, Nicolai II first thought of establishing a military dictatorship. Being reminded of the unreliability of the armed forces, he abandoned the plan. Some of his advisers suggested that the grant of a "constitution" might ultimately strengthen the autocracy. Accepting this advice, the emperor signed on October 30, 1905, a manifesto drafted by Witte, in which he promised to grant to the people unshakable foundations of civic freedom, inviolability of the person, freedom of conscience, freedom of speech, and the right of assembly. Henceforth no law could be passed without the agreement of an elected body called *duma*. In vague terms the manifesto proclaimed that suffrage for the duma would be a general and broad one, and that the deputies would have the possibility of participating in the supervision of the legality of executive actions. Through this manifesto the government gained a breathing spell. The unity of the revolutionary movement was broken. The right wing of the middle classes, led by Alexander Guchkov (1861-1936), who had fought with the Boers against Britain, accepted the manifesto and formed a party called "The Party of October." The liberals and the Mensheviks hoped that the manifesto would be the starting point for the development of a real constitutional monarchy after the Western model. The peasants and the workers were disappointed because the manifesto promised only political and personal liberty in which they were little interested and did not contain any program of social reforms. Nicolai II actually made some steps toward a very moderate constitutionalism: Pobyedonostsev was dismissed and Witte became Prime Minister; the balance owed by the peasants on their land which they had received at the time of the emancipation was canceled. A general strike proclaimed by the Moscow soviet in December, 1905, was put down by the government.

The revolutionary movement had lost its impetus. The government triumphed. It was now given the last chance to put itself at the head of a reform movement and of preparing Russia for an orderly transition from autocracy to liberty. Intoxicated by its apparent victory over the revolutionaries, the government failed to grasp the chance. It thereby precipitated a catastrophe which not only buried the tsarist government itself but Russian liberty too, and paved the way for the rise of a twentieth-century autocracy by far more efficient but also much more ruthless than any of the tsars.

— 6 —

THE SECOND LIBERAL PERIOD

1. The Constitution of 1906. The constitution promised in the October Manifesto of 1905 was promulgated on May 6, 1906. It was a strange constitution. It created a legislative assembly consisting of two houses of which the lower house, or duma, was elected on a practically universal suffrage. The two houses shared the legislative power with the emperor. But the emperor continued to be described in the constitution as "the supreme autocratic power," and, furthermore, "Acceptance of his authority is dictated not alone by fear and conscience but also by God Himself." Characteristically, "fear" was placed first in this official legitimation of the emperor's august position. This emphasis on autocracy established the new constitution as an unusually hybrid form of government, a constitutionally limited autocracy which amounts to a self-contradictory statement. In spite of this severe limitation, the duma possessed certain and in no way negligible powers, and if the duma had been allowed to go on and to function as expected in 1906, it might have created the foundations for the development of a constitutional and lawful regime in Russia. Yet this chance of permanency was not given, although the constitution, which was officially designated as the revised Fundamental Laws of the Russian Empire, explicitly set down the principle that the emperor had not the right of altering it without the agreement of the duma. Nevertheless, the constitution lasted less than two years. (*See Reading No. 19.*)

All in all, there were in the short span of ten years four elections for the duma. Each of the four dumas had its

own distinct personality. The elections to the first duma
were boycotted by the Social Revolutionary and the
Social Democratic Parties. Thus it came that the Kadets
represented the largest single group. On the whole, the
first duma showed a political complexion left of center.
The peasants and the national minorities were well represented. The new representatives could claim the confidence of the people, but they had no organizational
basis in the masses; on the other hand, they were unable
to establish any cooperation with the government, which
was determined to cling to the inviolability of the autocracy. Thus after only seventy-three days of existence,
the duma was dissolved on July 21, 1906, by imperial
order. The majority of the duma members—the Kadets
and the moderate Labor Party (*trudoviki*—the word
trud meaning labor)—went to Viborg in Finland across
the border in order to protest the dissolution of the duma
and to call in a manifesto upon the people to refuse cooperation with the government. But due to the lack of
any national or local organization at the grass roots, the
appeal of the progressive duma parties was not heeded.

A second duma was duly elected and showed an even
more leftist composition than the first. The socialist
groups participated this time, and though these leftist
parties did not elect more than about 100 deputies out
of 520, or less than one-fifth of the body, the extreme
rightist parties on which alone the government could
count for support were even smaller and disposed of not
more than 50 seats. Thus it was clear that no elections
based on a broad suffrage and freedom of vote would
produce a reactionary parliament according to the government's desire. Under these conditions the government
proceeded to an openly anti-constitutional *coup d'état*
by changing the electoral basis and methods without con-
sulting the duma or demanding its agreement as the constitution prescribed. The vote was practically taken away
from the peasants and the workers and, more significantly, from the national minorities. In addition, sufficient
pressure was exercised to secure a third duma which the
government found sufficiently amenable to its wishes
and ideas. The new duma was elected under the new
electoral law in 1907, and allowed to run its full constitutional term of five years. The fourth duma, elected

in 1912, was still in existence in 1917 when the revolution broke out. Not without justification did Sir Bernard Pares, a British student of Russian history, visualize the consequences of the emperor's *coup d'état* of 1907 as a factor in the development of 1917: "Ten years later in 1917, if Russia had possessed a duma elected by universal suffrage, it seems almost impossible that events would have followed the course which they actually took after the March Revolution of that year."

The third and fourth dumas counted a large preponderance of the wealthier classes, especially of the landowners, and, moreover, the parties of the right, which stood for the old principles of autocracy, orthodoxy, and a reactionary Russian nationalism, held more than one-fourth of the seats. The strongest single party was that of the moderately conservative Octobrists, willing to work under the existing constitution. The Kadets and the representatives of the workers were considerably reduced in numbers. Their importance grew, however, in the second half of the term of the fourth duma when the war emergency induced all the deputies except for the extreme right to form a progressive bloc. They united in demanding a more efficient cabinet that would enjoy the confidence of the country, without, however, insisting on a parliamentary cabinet responsible to the duma. The program which the progressive bloc put forward was characteristic of the most urgent needs of Russia as then understood by the large majority of Russian society: it called for the strict observance of the principle of legality in administration and for a consistent policy directed to the maintenance of internal peace and to the removal of racial and class antagonisms. The progressive bloc was convinced that these long-overdue reforms would strengthen the nation for a successful prosecution of the war then going on. These reforms might have averted the revolution. But the tsarist government rejected them and, as a sign of its hostility to even the moderate duma, closed its session. When the duma was called into session again at the end of 1916, it was too late. The country was in the throes of military defeat, administrative chaos, and despair over the existing conditions.

2. **Russia's Progress.** In spite of the curtailment of the powers of the duma, Russia in the 1910's was no

longer what she had been before 1905. Civic initiative
had been aroused. Despite the frequent introduction of
emergency measures and martial law, certain constitutional liberties were respected. Only the policy of persecu-
tion of national minorities, especially the Jews, remained
in full force and in some cases was even intensified.
The Union of the Russian people and the Union of the
Archangel Michael, supported by the Orthodox Church,
played an active role in anti-Semitic violence. There were
no more large-scale pogroms, but the arrest of Mendel
Beilis, a Jewish worker of Kiev, on the charge of ritual
murder of a Christian child, afforded an opportunity for
the government-supported anti-Semitic propaganda. The
subsequent famous trial drew the attention of the whole
world and ended with Beilis' acquittal for lack of evidence. Yet the fact that the government would press for
a trial on an absurd medieval charge such as ritual murder aroused a storm of protest throughout Russia, which
was voiced in meetings and in the press as it could never
have been before 1905. Thus the Beilis trial became one
of the points of crystallization in the struggle between reactionary autocracy and the forces trying to turn Russia
into a modern civilized country following the Western
model. After 1905, this struggle, which until then was
mostly underground, could be waged in the open. By
1914 Russia was successfully on the way to becoming a
full partner of the European community. In every field
of cultural and economic endeavor, Russia made great
progress from 1907 to 1914. During the decade preceding
the revolution, Russia lived through an era of rapidly
growing prosperity; culturally, the fight against illiteracy
was started with great vigor, and intellectual and artistic
relations with Europe became closer than ever before or
since.

3. Agrarian Reform. Economic progress made itself felt primarily in the rural areas as a result of the
agrarian reform embodied in successive legislations introduced by two Russian ministers, Peter Stolypin (1863-
1911), who was appointed Prime Minister in July, 1906,
and Vladimir Kokovtsov (1853-1943), who was Minister
of Finance from 1904 to 1914 and in 1911 became
Stolypin's successor as Prime Minister. Both were arch
conservatives and supported the autocracy, but among

the servants of the autocracy they were conspicuous for their intelligence, energy, and integrity. Their agrarian legislation aimed at increasing the personal rights of the peasants and at promoting the substitution of individual property for communal property. Not only communal arable land but also pastures and meadows could henceforth be divided, and the strips held by individual householders could be consolidated. Stolypin hoped thus to create an independent and prosperous farmers' class that would support the government against the urban intelligentsia and thus broaden the tenuous backing of the government in the country. Yet agriculture continued to suffer from lack of modern equipment and from low prices, especially compared with the high prices of industrial products. The prosperous farmers (kulaks) who worked efficiently remained a small minority, and village poverty continued. But there was an unmistakable change: the peasant, liberated from his legal incapacities, had the opportunity of buying land, of acquiring education, of producing more. The cooperative movement rapidly spread among the peasants. They grew more conscious of their political power and of their social cohesion. Russia's grain production rose from 580 million hundred weights in 1900 to 966 millions in 1913. Russia alone accounted for forty percent of the world export of cereals.

4. **Industrial Progress.** In the same years, Russia made equally great progress in the extraction of coal, iron ore, and oil and in the production of machinery and textiles. The main coal producing area was the Donets Basin in the eastern part of the Ukraine; iron ore was mined in the south and in the Ural Mountains; the center of the oil industry was at Baku and Grozny in the Caucasus. In 1913 Russia mined 360 million tons of coal as against 187 million in 1905; the iron ore production grew from 292 million pud (62 pud equal one ton) in 1905 to 507 million pud in 1913; the output of pig iron similarly expanded from 103 million pud in 1905 to 272 million pud in 1913. But far less spectacular was the growth of Russian oil extraction. It rose from 456 million pud in 1905 to 550 million pud in 1914, but due to the discovery of the great oil fields in southeastern Asia, Russia's share in world production fell from 37 percent in 1900 to 16

percent in 1913. In 1906 Russia produced only 20 thousand agricultural machines; by 1913 this figure, though still far below the requirements, had tripled. More important, however, than the rise of productivity was the general rise in the standard of living, which brought with it a growing self-assertiveness of the formerly often lethargic population.

This improvement of the Russian economy was helped by a stable currency, a balanced budget, and a large gold reserve, perhaps the largest in the world at that time. The deposits in commercial and savings banks rose rapidly: in the commercial banks they amounted to 1,165 million rubles in 1900, to 2,175 million in 1909, and to 3,952 million in 1912. In the same year, savings bank deposits amounted to 1,594 million rubles. Within five years the consumption of butter and sugar increased by about thirty percent. Mortality dropped from thirty-one per thousand in the period from 1901 to 1905 to twenty-six in 1911. The income from the postal, telephone, and telegraph services—which, as in all European countries, were monopolies of the state—more than doubled from 1903 to 1913. The consumption of paper grew from 252,000 tons in 1906 to 416,000 tons in 1912. Illiteracy among the younger generations was rapidly on the decline. In 1908 a program for the gradual and steady increase of the number of elementary schools was adopted with the goal of arriving at universal compulsory education by 1922. Among the army recruits the percentage of literacy with 49 in 1900 and 73 in 1914. The budget for the schools more than doubled in five years; it grew from 145 million rubles in 1909 to 328 million rubles five years later.

5. **Intellectual Development.** The increase in educational facilities did not mean, however, that Russia as a whole had reached European levels by 1914. In the rural districts where more than four-fifths of the Russian population lived, European ways of life and true literacy had hardly penetrated. Many of the young peasants who had gone to school for a few years did not make great use of their ability to read and write after they left school. The situation was different in the larger cities, especially in St. Petersburg, by far the most Europeanized center of Russian life. There even the court and the aristocracy,

with their many close relations abroad, served as a factor which helped to overcome Russian isolationism and traditionalism. In comparison, Moscow was much more remote, provincial, and Russian. This city often consciously represented Russian "nationalism" as against the "cosmopolitan" capital. But in all the larger cities and in many isolated country manors there was a rapidly growing educated class in close touch with European cultural trends. Some Russian newspapers and, above all, the influential Russian monthly and quarterly periodicals equaled in quality the best in the Western world. Though censorship and emergency legislation continued, they interfered much less than before with the freedom of press and printing. Books and newspapers represented all shades of public opinion including Marxist and other leftist doctrines. Public discussion of political and cultural problems was lively and open. The Bolshevik Party could start the publication of its official organ *Pravda* (*Truth*) as a daily in St. Petersburg in Apil, 1912. A Russian millionaire provided the necessary funds.

The modicum of liberty which the regime allowed after 1905 and the increased intercourse with Europe intensely stimulated Russian intellectual life. The latest and most advanced trends in Western art were quickly adopted in Russia, and Russian art, beyond the long-established influence of the novel, began on its part to stimulate and fertilize Western cultural development. The seclusion and exclusiveness characteristic of the Russian mind for many centuries seemed definitely on the way out. The large majority of the educated classes participated fully in the common cultural development of the continent. Yet a gulf still separated this educated class from the Russian masses who did not yet fully appreciate the struggle for liberty under law and the education toward legal concepts and rights which marked the period from 1905 to 1917. This split of Russia into two nations who hardly shared a common language or a common way of life helped to divert the Russian Revolution in 1917 from its hopeful beginnings and was one of the fundamental causes responsible for the destruction of the short-lived liberty which the revolution had brought into being. The peasants were unwilling to follow the liberal and Westernized urban classes whom they distrusted. The war of 1914 and the almost absurd ineptitude of the government precipitated a revolutionary development long before Russia, with its vast multitudes dispersed over its endless spaces, was prepared for liberty.

6. **The New Literary Movement.** The three outstanding writers of Russia at the beginning of the twentieth century were Anton Chekhov (1860-1904), Maxim Gorky (1869-1936), and Ivan Bunin (1870-1953). Each represented a different stage in the development of Russian letters. Chekhov, who has become more famous abroad for his plays but holds a unique position in the hearts of Russian readers as a writer of short stories, can be considered the last great nineteenth-century Russian writer. His works are still variations on the melancholy theme of the superfluous man and convey the atmosphere of the purposelessness of a stagnant society. His main theme, to quote D. S. Mirsky, is "the mutual unsurpassable isolation of human beings and the impossibility of understanding each other." His heroes are deeply disillusioned with life, their own lives, and life in general. The same mood of depression and the same minute attention to psychological detail in which his short stories excel are characteristic of his plays of which *The Three Sisters* and *The Cherry Orchard* have gained a firm place in Western repertory. Gorky was in every respect different from Chekhov. In his background and in his mood, Gorky belonged to a new generation. Though Chekhov's father had been born a serf, he had become a well-to-do merchant and thus could give his son an excellent education. Chekhov was by training a physician, though he did not practice his profession. Gorky, on the other hand, was a self-made man who had worked his way up from the lowest level of society to become at the early age of thirty a writer as famous abroad as in Russia.

In his early teens, Gorky lived as a tramp wandering over the endless roads of Russia where he met all sorts of people from "the nether depths"—later to be the title of one of his plays (1902) which was performed many hundreds of times in Moscow and Berlin. Gorky no longer depicted the hopeless fatigue of Chekhov's generation but the defiant attitude of men who break away from a stagnant society and sense the storm-warnings of a new era. His novels offer the vast panorama of backward provincial Russia with which he was thoroughly familiar. The later ones are marred by moralizing and much too lengthy conversations, but his first one, *Foma Gordeev* (1899), is a vivid tale, "the constructive and masculine spirit of which gives it a flavor rare in Russian literature." At the time of writing this novel, Gorky became a member of the Social Democratic Party and founded a publishing house to which he gave the characteristic name *Znanye* (*Knowledge*). It promoted a school of revolutionary realism in literature and dedicated itself to the dissemination of popular books on science and practical knowledge. Gorky took a prominent part in the revolution of 1905 and, though he had many misgivings about the Bolsheviks, he joined them after his return to Russia in 1928. He became the official father of the school called "socialist realism," which in 1934 became the only recognized form of Soviet art. Two years later, in the period of the great purges, Gorky died under strange circumstances, perhaps because Stalin no longer felt certain of his "loyalty."

Bunin, less known abroad than Chekhov or Gorky, was the only Russian writer ever to receive the Nobel Prize for Literature. This happened in 1933, twenty years after the publication of his first great novel, the somberly realistic *Village* (1910). This work, which he wrote as a member of Gorky's *Znanye* group, is an indictment of backward Russian peasantry without any of the customary idealizing of the "good people." Bunin shared neither Gorky's political radicalism nor his effusiveness of style. His best known story *The Gentleman from San Francisco* (1916) is a masterpiece of terseness. It deals with a theme which is neither Russian nor social, but eternal: the loneliness and helplessness of man in the presence of death. In 1918 Bunin took a strong anti-Bolshevik stand and left Russia never to return.

Less known abroad than these three prose writers but perhaps equally important for Russia was the rise of a new school of poetry. Under the influence of French symbolism and of Nietzsche, the old moralistic views of social utilitarianism which had influenced much of nineteenth-century Russian writing and which later were revived in an exaggerated form by the Bolshevik school of socialist realism, gave way to an emphasis on esthetic

values and form. In that way, Russian letters at the beginning of the twentieth century became an integral part of
the general European literature of the period. To quote
Mirsky again, "estheticism substituted beauty for duty,
and individualism emancipated the individual from all
social obligations." A new feeling for form and for
artistic culture in itself was awakened; a hopeful fermentation in all fields of cultural endeavor set in which
persisted into the first years of the Bolshevik regime
when it was stamped out by the communist autocracy.

Among the new poets, Valery Bryusov (1873-1924),
Alexander Blok (1880-1921), Sergei Esenin (1895-
1925), and Vladimir Mayakovsky (1894-1930) were
perhaps the best known. Some of them were filled with
a vague religious or patriotic messianism which made
them welcome Lenin's revolution. They were not interested in its social and political ideas, but interpreted it
in its esthetic apocalyptic aspects as an immense pas-
sionate upheaval which would renew the face of the
earth through the elemental forces of a wild fire. Bryusov
hailed the revolution as an "ocean of a people's wrath,"
and Blok saw it for a short time as a purifying blizzard
cleansing the world. In the terrible winter of 1917-18
Blok wrote two famous poems. The first of them, *The
Twelve,* was repeatedly translated into most European
languages. It is a masterpiece of power and music in
language. It ends with the vision of the figure of Christ
who appears among twelve rough Red guardsmen lurch-
ing at night through the streets of St. Petersburg in a
blinding snow storm. The second poem, *The Scythians,*
called upon the Western peoples to join communist Russia in a common effort toward building a new world; in
case they should refuse to do it, the poet threatened
them with the coming onrush of Asian hordes who would
destroy the civilization of the West. After Lenin's seizure
of power, Bryusov and Blok stayed on in Russia but
they outlived Lenin's whirlwind for only a very short
time and died, lonely and disappointed men.

Esenin and Mayakovsky were of a younger and more
aggressive generation. Esenin, whom Gorky once called
Russia's greatest lyrical genius since Pushkin, spoke of
himself in his poems as a hooligan. His short and unhappy marriage to the American dancer Isadora Duncan

made him better known abroad than his hardly translatable poems, which, like the poems of this whole new
artistic movement, have an immensely musical texture,
and enriched the Russian language through new experiments. By far less musical was Mayakovsky who, as a
"futurist," broke with all poetical traditions. He became
the official mouthpiece of the revolution, its "loud-
speaker," the conscious writer of effective propaganda
poetry. In an early poem "150,000,000," he anticipated
a decisive struggle between communist Russia and capitalist America, and depicted the colossal figure of the
peasant Ivan, the champion of communism, wading
across the Atlantic to fight Woodrow Wilson, the champion of plutocracy. Both poets, Esenin and Mayakovsky,
died in their early manhood by suicide, unhappy lost
souls of a period which had seemed to them one of
blazing promise but in which there was room for neither
artistic creativeness nor for individual happiness.

7. **The Flowering of Art.** The twenty years before
Lenin's seizure of power had witnessed in many fields
besides literature an unprecedented flowering of the artistic genius of the Russian people. Art for art's sake
became the program of the beautiful periodical *Mir
Iskustva* (*The World of Art*) which was founded in
1898 by Sergei Diaghilev (1872-1929) who was famous
not only as an art critic but, above all, as a ballet producer. He became the most important single interme-
diary between Russian and Western esthetic culture; he
brought modern art to Russia and Russian art to Europe. It is probably no overstatement to say that in this
enterprise, Diaghilev helped to renew the art of ballet
in Western Europe and to raise it to a new level of artistic splendor. The Russian Imperial Ballet which he
was the first to bring to Europe in 1909 combined bold
color backgrounds, unconventional music, dramatic emphasis, and technical perfection. Among Diaghilev's
choreographers was Michel Fokine (1880-1942) who
created "The Death of the Swan" for the celebrated
dancer Anna Pavlova (1885-1931). Diaghilev's most
famous male dancer was Waslaw Nijinsky (1890-1950).
A name of equal importance connected with the Russian
ballet was Leon Bakst (1866-1924) who was the chief
designer of Russian stage settings. Later in Paris, Diaghi-

lev used not only Russian artists but also the foremost of the European vanguard, like Picasso and Derain among the painters, Milhaud and Poulenc among the musicians. It was in Paris that Diaghilev met the young Russian composer Igor Stravinsky (b. 1882), a disciple of Rimsky-Korsakov; and it was for Diaghilev's ballet that Stravinsky wrote his most famous early compositions *The Fire Bird* (1910), *Petrushka* (1912), *The Rite of Spring* (1913), and *The Nightingale* (1914), works that, through their originality and force, exercised a wide influence on young composers everywhere. Diaghilev also organized the first exhibition of modern French painting in St. Petersburg and of Russian painting in Paris. At the same time rich Moscow merchants, the Tretiakovs, the Shchukins, and Ivan Morozov, built up private collections of modern French paintings which belonged to the best in the world.

From this interplay between Russia and Europe in the cultural field, the theater, always a favorite of the Russian public, benefited too. Until 1882 a government monopoly of all theaters in Russia had existed. The abrogation of this monopoly allowed free experiment, and individual genius and the Russian stage itself matched European standards and grew in importance. The new theater movement in Russia coincided with a general European trend that expressed itself in the French *Théâtre Libre* founded by André Antoine in Paris in 1887 and in the *Freie Bühne* in Berlin, which became at that time the home for the works of Henrik Ibsen and Gerhart Hauptmann. In 1898 Konstantine Stanislavsky (1863-1938) followed their example in founding his Moscow Art Theater which in its first season produced Chekhov's *Seagull* and made it a great success. Another Russian producer who influenced the development of the modern stage was Vsevolod Meyerhold (1874-1940). As Stanislavsky's major rival, he led the opposition to the realistic theater developed by Stanislavsky to its highest standards. He was not so much bent on a faithful presentation of the play as he was on its imaginative adaptation to the theater, which he regarded as an art form in itself. He was a champion of creative and imaginative experiments using the theater as a laboratory, removing all scenery and props, pro-

ducing effects by new ways of lighting, and trying to
induce the audience to an active participation in the
basic or essential feeling of the play. He courageously
defended his art against Bolshevik regimentation and
disappeared in a concentration camp where he probably
was killed. But with the restoration of the governmental
monopoly of theatrical life in the fully developed Bolshevik regime, the marvelous effervescence of the theater,
as well as of Russian intellectual and cultural life in
general, which had characterized the preceding two decades came to an end.

8. **Governmental Decadence.** The great progress
which Russia's economic and cultural development
showed led Russian society to reject even more strongly
the ineffectual and disintegrating administration which
centered in an impotent autocracy. The loss of prestige
suffered by Russia through defeat in the Japanese war
deeply rankled in the minds of the educated classes and
did not enhance the authority of the court in their circles. Things grew rapidly worse as the result of an unexpected development attending the birth in August,
1904, during the war, of the long-awaited male heir to
the throne. It was soon discovered that Alexei suffered
from hemophilia, an incurable disease. All medical treatment was to no avail. The empress, who had always
shown a mystical streak, turned to miracle workers in
her desperate attempts to cure the young heir. A Siberian peasant, Gregory Rasputin (1871-1916), apparently was able to help the boy. Rasputin was neither a
priest nor a monk but a "miracle-working saintly" man.
Yet at the same time he was what his name meant, for
the name Rasputin was a nickname given him by his
fellow peasants and signified "the dissolute." But in Russia, extreme dissolution if followed by extreme repentance did not necessarily diminish Rasputin's position;
undoubtedly he possessed great natural intelligence, and
in his apparent simplicity he seemed to represent the imperial
couple to represent the mystical truly Russian being: a
man of God and at the same time a typical man of the
people. The unsavory side of his character—excessive
drunkenness, sexual orgies, and rapacious greed—apparently remained unknown to the imperial family.

No criticism of Rasputin was allowed to reach the

emperor, and his confidence in his wife's judgment and
in Rasputin remained unshaken. This could happen because the couple, largely due to their shyness and self-
sufficiency, lived a very isolated life, isolated not only
from Russian society but even from the high aristocracy
and their own relatives. The emperor's own reactionary
ministers, wise enough to advise the emperor to send
Rasputin away, were not heeded. They fell into disgrace.
To the imperial couple, Rasputin represented the simple God-fearing peasants, on the union with whom the
strength of the autocracy was supposed to rest. Thus
they eagerly listened to his advice. Rasputin had neither
direct political ambitions nor any political philosophy;
he had only the insatiable demand and the capacity for
endless orgies. He understood that he could satisfy his
inclinations through the favor of the imperial family
and the power which this favor gave him. Thus he was
vitally interested in the strictest preservation of unlimited
autocracy. For entirely different reasons the empress
shared this goal; she wished to preserve the inherited
autocratic power in its fullest splendor for her beloved
husband and their only son. To the empress and to Rasputin the slightest constitutional reform seemed to spell
the end of their cherished ideals. In such a strange way,
a man of keen intellect and extreme dissoluteness of
character and a woman of an exactly opposite character
and mind worked unwittingly together toward the destruction of the very regime which they were so eager
to preserve.

In this atmosphere even intelligent conservatives like
Stolypin and Kokovstov could not count on support by
the emperor. Kokovstov was dismissed from office in
January, 1914. It was upon Rasputin's recommendation
that Ivan Goremykin (1839-1918) was appointed Prime
Minister, a helpless and colorless reactionary, whose
vitality had not increased with his years. He was an easy
tool in Rasputin's hands. The calamity which this sinister
control foreshadowed became more manifest during
Goremykin's term of office when Russia entered the
First World War. She waged the war on the side of the
constitutional democracies of the West; she could pursue
the war successfully only if the government was supported by public opinion and enjoyed its confidence. Of

both these factors the imperial couple took no cogni-
zance. The narrow-minded but strong-willed empress
steeled her weaker husband against any concessions whatever to Western ways of government or to public demands for reform. The letters which she sent him at
the army headquarters show a strange blend of an almost
bride-like affection in a middle-aged woman and a domi-
neering insistence upon unlimited autocracy. Their correspondence was always in English. "My very own beloved One," she wrote on August 22, 1915, "Do not
fear for what remains behind—one must be severe and
stop all advance. Lovy, I am here, don't laugh at silly
old wify, but she has [*trousers*] on unseen, and I can
get the old man to come and keep him up to be energetic—whenever I can be of the smallest use, tell me
what to do—use me—at such a time God will give me
the strength to help you—because our souls are fighting
for the right against evil. It is all much deeper than it
appears to the eye—we, who have been taught to look
at all from another side, see what the struggle really is
and means—you showing your mastery, proving yourself the *Autocrat* without whom Russia cannot exist."
She implored him to remain firm and not to make the
slightest concession. She assured him that God would
not forsake His anointed, and that "our Friend's (Rasputin's) prayers arise night and day for you to Heaven
and God will hear them." God apparently did not.
Timely concessions to the rising claims for reforms might
have helped much more to halt the rapid decay of governmental authority than Rasputin's prayers.

9. **The Revolutionary Movement.** The apparent
success of the autocracy in reestablishing itself firmly in
1906 and 1907 produced deep discouragement among
the revolutionary youth. It sought escape, for the time
being, in sensual dissipation, of which Mikhail Artsyba-
shev (1878-1927) gave a picture in his novel *Sanin*
(1907) which had a short-lived vogue in Russia and
abroad. Former Marxists like Sergei Bulgakov (1871-
1944) and Nicolai Berdyayev (1874-1948) turned to
Orthodoxy and became Russia's foremost religious thinkers. They were among the seven authors of the famous
collection of essays which appeared in 1909 under the
title *Vekhy* (*Guideposts*). They appealed for a new un-

derstanding of Russian history and opposed the lack of
religion and patriotism among many of the revolutionary
intellectuals. The period of discouragement ended, however, around 1910. Like always, several factors cooperated in producing the changed mood. For one, the death
of Tolstoy, whose powerful voice had frequently protested against the excesses of governmental repression,
aroused the youth. His death came during his dramatic
flight from home at a little railroad station in November,
1910; with Tolstoy, the last great nineteenth-century
moral figure disappeared from the scene.

On the other hand, the labor movement was steadily
growing in strength. By 1901, three million workers were
employed in mines and factories, and though strikes were
illegal and the law kept trade-union activities within nar-
row bounds, their existence helped form a sense of solidarity among the workers and to train their potential
leaders. Thus they were able to secure the health and
accident insurance law of 1912 and to achieve small
but steady wage gains. The Russian trade-union movement was well on the way to becoming an instrument of
social progress as the Mensheviks hoped it would, and
they expected it to replace the conspiratorial revolutionary activities on which the Bolsheviks relied. Labor unrest rose rapidly after April, 1912, the date of a strike
in the Lena gold fields of Siberia, which was severely
repressed with a large number of casualties. As a result,
workers throughout the country staged sympathy strikes.
In the two and one half years before the outbreak of the
war there were more than six thousand strikes, involving
in 1914 alone 1,450,000 workers. Strikes were frequent
in the metal and textile industries. After 1910 the revolutionary activity also led to the resumption of terrorism.
Stolypin himself was assassinated at a gala performance
in the Kiev opera house on September 14, 1911. The
unsatisfactory situation at home, which deprived Russia
from taking its place among the free people of Europe
and thus humiliated the growing self-awareness of Russian society, had its consequences in another field: many
shades of Russian public opinion sought compensation
in a bold attitude in foreign affairs which would restore
Russian prestige and satisfy national self-confidence.

10. Foreign Policy.   Russia emerged from the war

with Japan with lowered military prestige and with practically its whole fleet destroyed. The government thus devoted much effort to the restoration of Russia's armed forces. After 1908, Russian artillery was considerably improved and modernized and the fulfillment of the rearmament program was anticipated by 1917. After her defeat by the Japanese, Russia abandoned, at least for the time being, her plans in the Far East. An agreement with Japan in 1907 removed the dangers of conflict in that area. Of even greater importance for Russia's Asian and European policy was Russia's entente of August, 1907, with Britain. It settled the century-old rivalry between the two powers in Asia through an agreement on the most important points of dispute. Persia was divided into a Russian sphere of influence in the north, which included the capital city of Teheran, and a British sphere in the south, which included the oil fields and access to the Persian Gulf. The Russians renounced their aspirations in Afghanistan and the British on their part promised to withdraw from Tibet, the independence of which was to be respected by both parties. These settlements in central and eastern Asia gave Russia the opportunity of turning her attention to the Near East—the Balkans and Turkey—where she hoped for an opportunity of realizing her aspirations of the last two centuries.

Important events changed the political picture in the Balkan peninsula from that which the Congress of Berlin had established in 1878. In 1908, the Young Turks assumed control of Turkey in the hope of reforming and strengthening the disintegrating empire; Austria-Hungary annexed the two Slav-speaking, formerly Turkish provinces of Bosnia-Herzegovina, an area which it had administered since 1878. This annexation aroused the bitter resentment of the neighboring Serbs, a Slav people of the Orthodox faith, who looked to Russia for support. But Russia was at that moment still too weak to oppose Austria-Hungary, which was backed by Germany. Russian public opinion profoundly resented this "humiliation." Alexander Izvolsky (1856-1919), who had been Minister of Foreign Affairs from 1906 on, was sent as Ambassador to France in 1910 to strengthen the Franco-Russian alliance. Stolypin's son-in-law Sergei Sazonov

(1866-1927) became Minister of Foreign Affairs in his
stead. Russian diplomacy became very active in the Balkans and sponsored military agreements among the four
Christian Balkan kingdoms—Serbia, Bulgaria, Greece,
and Montenegro—but these nations, in their own aggressive nationalism, precipitated events beyond Russia's
plans. In October, 1912, they attacked Turkey to "liberate" Turkish provinces with large Christian populations, principally Macedonia. A few months later they
fought each other bitterly over the disposition of the
"liberated" regions. Serbia and Greece emerged from
the war with greatly increased territories and greatly en-
hanced self-confidence. On the other hand, Bulgaria was
defeated by its former allies and was deprived of any
gain from the war with Turkey. Looking for revenge,
Bulgaria sought the support of Austria-Hungary, whereas
the Serbs relied upon Russian and French backing, not
only in order to keep their great territorial gains from
the war with Turkey but also to make similar gains at
the expense of Austria-Hungary. They regarded themselves as the Balkan Piedmont or Prussia, the military
spearhead of a unification of all southern Slavs under
Serb leadership, a goal which could be achieved only
through the disintegration of Austria-Hungary. Thus by
1913, the Balkans had become the explosive powder-
keg of European diplomacy.

The spark was supplied on June 28, 1914 by the assassination of the Austrian heir to the throne, Archduke
Francis Ferdinand, by Serbian terrorist youths in Sara-
jevo, the capital of Bosnia. Austria-Hungary accused
Serbia of complicity with the secret organization which
had plotted the assassination, and resented the Pan Slav
propaganda by Serbian and Russian agents which aimed
at undermining the loyalty of Austria-Hungary's Slav
inhabitants. This propaganda seemed especially effective
among the southern Slavs, the Croats and Slovenes, living near the Serbian borders. The Austrian general staff
believed that Austria must act to destroy Serbia's hostile
intentions before Russia was fully rearmed and could
effectively uphold Serbia. The German general staff fully
supported this Austrian determination to settle accounts
with Serbia. The war of 1914 broke out largely as a re-

sult of what might be vaguely called Pan German and
Pan Slav aspirations and fears. When Austria tried to
impose its will on Serbia, Russia decided not to abandon
the Slav and Orthodox nation. Russian public opinion,
as expressed in the duma and in the press, not only
supported the government but was even more determined than the court to uphold Slav solidarity and Russia's great power position. The Russian educated classes
also expected a favorable domestic development as a
result of the war, for they were certain that the government would be forced to call for a more active participation of the people in national life to enable a successful prosecution of the war. By assuming responsible
positions in the direction of the war effort, the educated
classes would gain influence and Russia would inevitably
be changed into a constitutional and liberal state, after
the example of its Western allies. It was widely believed
that the war would achieve what the revolution of 1905
had not achieved—an end to the obsolete autocratic
form of government in Russia.

Only few influential persons were strongly opposed to
Russia fighting a war on behalf of Serbia; among them
was Count Witte. In the duma, only the Bolsheviks opposed the war. They expressed their faith in the solidarity
of the proletariat of all the countries, and declared that
the war was a struggle between "imperialists and brig-
ands." In their illegal proclamations they favored the
defeat of Russia as a means of bringing the Russian
proletariat to power and called for the fraternization of
the Russians on the front with the enemy and the preparation of an uprising at home. Except for these small
groups, the government at the outset of the war was
not only backed by public opinion but found itself on
the crest of a wave of popularity as never before. Soon,
however, this popularity completely vanished. The government was not only accused of inefficiency and corruption, but it was felt that its leadership in itself en-
dangered the fatherland and was a hindrance to success
at home and abroad. Mutual confidence between the
patriotic people and their government was absent after
the first days of enthusiasm, and this gulf steadily widened. The patriots were incensed; the workers and the
peasants were indifferent; the government and the coun-

try disintegrated under a war effort for which they were neither morally nor economically prepared. Thus the soil was prepared for the revolution of March, 1917.

— 7 —

PROMISE AND FAILURE

1. **The Beginning of the War.** The Russian army fought in the first months of the war with great courage and not without success. Soon, however, the deficiencies in equipment, the incompetence of the high leadership, and the backward state of communications made themselves adversely felt. Like most statesmen and generals of the time, the Russian leadership did not expect a protracted war. The Russian Minister of War Vladimir Sukhomlinov (1848-1926) was convinced that the Russian munition supplies—three times larger than those used against Japan—would be sufficient for the war which he foresaw. Later on he was held responsible for the country's military unpreparedness at the outbreak of the war; many of his adversaries suspected not only incompetence but treason. Nor was the appointment of Grand Duke Nicolai (1856-1929), a grandson of Tsar Nicolai I, as Commander in Chief a fortunate choice. The Russians were forced into action before they were ready. The Germans concentrated their forces first against France and wished to remain purely on the defensive in the east. But due to French pressure for a "second front," Russian cavalry was sent into eastern Prussia where at the end of August they suffered a heavy defeat by the Germans under the command of Paul von Hindenburg. More successful was the Russian army which was led by General Alexei Brusilov (1853-1926) and which in the winter of 1914-15 conquered almost

the whole of Austrian Galicia. It even succeeded in occupying the crest of the Carpathian Mountains. From
this point it threatened to descend into the plains of
Hungary and to march on the Hungarian capital of
Budapest. If that had happened, the Russians might have
defeated Austria-Hungary in the spring of 1915 and isolated Germany.

But the Russian offensive was halted, German armies
were moved in the late spring of 1915 to the eastern
front, and assumed the offensive. Together with the Aus-
trians in the summer and fall of 1915 they occupied the
whole of Poland and some of the western provinces of
Russia. This disaster and the great losses which the
Russian army suffered aroused a bitter public feeling of
disappointment in the interior. It became known that
the Russian soldiers were forced to meet the onslaught
of the well-equipped German forces not only with in-
sufficient support by aircraft and artillery but often,
among the newly arrived reserves, without even sufficient
rifles or shoes. The consternation turned into panic when
in an ill-advised moment the emperor decided in August,
1915, to assume the supreme command himself. Grand
Duke Nicolai was sent as commander in chief to the
Caucasian front to fight against the Turks who in the
fall of 1914 had entered the war on the side of Germany.

It was well known that the emperor was no military
leader; on the other hand it was felt that he, being the
autocrat on whom all government depended, was needed
in the capital. But the emperor was glad to escape responsibility. He left the capital so that he might see as
little as possible of his own ministers and the political
leaders, and that he might lead the "simple life" which
he liked among the selected company at his headquarters.
Meanwhile, the empress remained in the capital to look
after the affairs of state. In all her decisions she obeyed
her own reactionary inspiration and refused any contact
with the nation in the most critical periods of the war.

The patriotic wave which had swept much of the
country at the beginning of the war had not yet sub-
sided. The *zemstvos* and civic organizations of all kinds
were working energetically for a more rapid move of
supplies to the front and for the improvement of do-

mestic conditions. Though the duma was adjourned after the one-day session of August 8, 1914, during which it had voted the war credits, it continued to function informally as a committee for the relief of war suffering under the chairmanship of its president Mikhail Rodzianko (1859-1924). A War Industries Committee under the chairmanship of Alexander Guchkov (1861-1936), a former president of the duma, tried to mobilize and coordinate the industrial effort. All these men were conservatives who were driven into opposition to the government not for any revolutionary motives but out of pure patriotism. As a result of their labor, the Russian army was better equipped in 1916 than at the beginning of the war, though it still remained greatly inferior to the German army. Under these conditions, Brusilov undertook to start a new offensive on the southern end of the front, partly to relieve Austrian pressure on Italy. After some initial successes, however, the offensive was stopped and the Russian army suffered a large number of casualties which undermined its morale. The discouraging conditions at the front were aggravated by the rising discontent of the poorer classes throughout the empire. The transportation system, always one of the weak elements in the vast country, was unable to move foodstuffs and fuel to the big cities. Important industrial districts situated in the western part of the empire had fallen into German hands.

The situation could have been alleviated if the western allies had been able to supply Russia with industrial products and ammunition. For that purpose Winston Churchill had planned the famous expedition to the Dardanelles to force a passage into the Black Sea. The campaign, however, known in history as the Gallipoli expedition, failed. Perhaps if it had succeeded, Russia might have stayed in the war until the Western victory, and the necessary revolutionary changes could have taken place under much more favorable conditions. Only the northern ports of Murmansk and Arkhangelsk remained for the purpose of Western and Russian contact and they were of little use. Arkhangelsk had flourished as the sole Russian seaport until the time of Peter the Great, but the harbor was sometimes closed for more than six months of the year by ice. Murmansk, although ice-free, was connected by railroad with the interior only during the latter part of the war when there was not sufficient railroad stock in any case. A large part of the railroad material had fallen into German hands and the lack of raw material and skilled workers reduced the output of the factories below the prewar level.

For lack of hands, agriculture, too, suffered. As a result of more than thirteen million soldiers having been called into service, only women and old men remained on many of the peasant farms, and the estates were unable to find hired farm hands. But the cities suffered even more than the countryside. The rising inflation drove prices up without a corresponding increase in wages. This inflation resulted from the enormous expenditures of war. The war effort cost 1,820 million rubles in 1915 and 14,573 million rubles in 1916, almost eight times as much. At the beginning of the war, banknotes in circulation amounted to 1,630 million rubles; on January 1, 1917, the figure had risen more than five times to 9,103 million rubles. Prices had risen even more sharply and the increase became catastrophic during 1916. The price index rose from 100 at the outbreak of the war to 115 on January 1, 1915, to 238 on January 1, 1916, and it jumped to 702 by January 1, 1917. In this critical time, the tsar dismissed the helpless and extremely reactionary Goremykin, but did not appoint men capable of dealing with the situation; Goremykin's successors were even more despised and detested by the whole of Russia than he had been. Boris Stürmer (1849-1917), who became Prime Minister and Foreign Minister, Alexander Trepov (1863-1928) who succeeded him in November, 1916, and Alexander Protopopov (1864-1918), who was Minister of the Interior under these two premiers, were openly accused of treason because it seemed unbelievable that they should have taken measures which clearly aggravated the catastrophic situation only out of sheer stupidity and corruption.

2. The Revolutionary Duma. By this time it had become manifest that things could no longer go on in the old way. The revolutionary mood was in the air. The only questions which remained to be decided were whether revolution would come from above or from below, and whether it could be postponed until after the

war or whether it would erupt in the midst of the war. The duma was now practically united on the need for a thorough change of the government. That was true even of the more intelligent leaders of the extreme right like the fanatical Vladimir Purishkevich, the founder of the infamous Union of the Archangel Michael which had organized or supported pogroms and other sinister and criminal exploits. When the duma was again called into session on November, 1916, Purishkevich joined Milyukov, the leader of the progressive Kadets, in denouncing the government in the most outspoken fashion. The high nobility thought even of a palace revolution of the kind that had been current in Russia before the modern period and of which the last example had been the assassination of Tsar Paul I by high-ranking court officers in 1801. Nothing came of these plans except the murder of Rasputin who was invited at the end of December to an orgy in the palace of Prince Felix Yusupov. Among the party which did away with him was the Grand Duke Dmitri, a nephew of the emperor, and Purishkevich.

But, as Professor Florinsky rightly points out, the removal of Rasputin did little to influence or appease the revolutionary temper of the country. The masses did not hate Rasputin but "the inequities of Russia's political, social, and economic structure, and the additional burden thrust upon the country by the exigencies of a great war. Rasputin was a symptom, not the cause, of a pathological condition that led the monarchy to its doom." In the duma, one of the right-wing liberals—a conservative by all Western standards—Basil Maklakov, declared that it could not be a simple accident that the few ministers who enjoyed the confidence of the country were dismissed, whereas the ministers hated by the nation were confirmed in their office. "No! That is no accident," he cried out, "it is the regime itself, that cursed old regime, which is obsolete but still lives on. The old regime and the interests of Russia have now parted company; and every minister is faced with the dilemma whether he wishes to serve Russia or serve the regime. Woe to that country," he concluded, quoting Pushkin, "where only the slave and the liar are close to the throne." This attitude of the duma understand-

ably upset the empress, but it did not make her realize
the seriousness of the situation. She described the members of the duma as "impertinent brutes," declared that
there was a war going on between the duma and the
imperial couple, and exhorted the emperor to crush them
all and to send their leaders to Siberia.

3. The Allies and Russia. The situation in Russia
was naturally viewed with deep concern by the Western
Allies. In the winter of 1916-17 the situation at the
western front was in no way favorable to the allies, and
Germany was about to declare unlimited submarine war-
fare against Britain. The British ambassador, Sir George
Buchanan (1854-1924), who had been at his post in St.
Petersburg since 1910, described in his *My Mission to
Russia* an audience with the emperor in January, 1917,
in which he implored the monarch "to break down the
barrier that separates you from your people and to regain their confidence." The emperor resented this sug-
gestion, but Buchanan went on with the following pro-
phetic words: "Your Majesty must remember that the
people and the army are but one, and that in the event
of a revolution only a small portion of the army can be
counted on to defend the dynasty. An Ambassador, I
am well aware, has no right to hold the language which
I have held to Your Majesty, and I had to take my
courage in both hands before speaking as I have done.
I can but plead as my excuse the fact that I have throughout been inspired by my feelings of devotion for Your
Majesty and the Empress. If I were to see a friend walk-
ing through a wood on a dark night along a path which
I knew ended in a precipice, would it not be my duty,
Sir, to warn him of his danger? And is it not equally
my duty to warn Your Majesty of the abyss that lies
ahead of you? You have, Sir, come to the parting of the
ways, and you have now to choose between two paths.
The one will lead you to victory and a glorious peace—
the other to revolution and disaster. Let me implore
Your Majesty to choose the former. By following it you
will, Sir, secure for your country the realization of its
secular ambitions and for yourself the position of the
most powerful Sovereign in Europe. But above all else,
Your Majesty will assure the safety of those who are

dear to you and be free from all anxiety on their account."

But no intervention, be it by Russian patriots or by Allied friends, was able to make the tsar see the danger ahead. Even if he had seen it, it was probably too late. The regime was thoroughly discredited. Influential duma circles still hoped for a constitutional monarchy after the abdication of the emperor, upon which they all were agreed. But the masses did not care for any program or plan. They were simply fed up with the whole thing and there was no efficient governmental force in being to check their elemental desires. Thus the March Revolution of 1917 came about. It not only destroyed tsardom but, as Buchanan had foreseen, cost the tsar and all those dear to him their lives.

4. The March Revolution. The revolution broke out without leadership and without any preconceived plan. In its preparation or in its initial stages, Lenin and the Bolsheviks played no role whatever. At the beginning of 1917, Lenin and Trotsky were both abroad. During his exile in Switzerland, Lenin had agitated violently against the "imperialist" war. Supported by a few extremists from other countries, he organized in September, 1915, a conference at Zimmerwald. This conference released a manifesto which called upon the workers of all nations at war to overthrow their own governments and to transform the national war into an international class war. The appeal made hardly any impression on the working classes, nor did it penetrate to the Russian masses. They were moved by much more primitive instincts than Marxist teachings. Lenin himself had no clear vision of the future or any astonishing farsightedness. In January, 1917, when practically everybody sensed the imminence of the Russian revolution, Lenin assured a Zurich audience that men of his generation were not likely to "live to see the decisive events of the approaching revolution." (*See Reading No. 20.*) When, within a few weeks, reality proved him wrong, he adapted himself very quickly to the unforeseen and boldly asserted the very opposite, telling the Swiss workers that the Russian events were the beginning of a socialist revolution throughout Europe and that the trans-

formation of the imperialist war into an international civil war, as he had foreseen it, was now becoming a fact.

The revolution broke out not only unexpected by Lenin but without any theoretical guidance by anyone else. It was not engendered by political leaders, socialist theoreticians, or liberal intellectuals. It started in St. Petersburg on March 8 and 9 with spontaneous hunger demonstrations of factory workers, mostly women. The government tried to stop these demonstrations, but a corresponding order to the troops on Sunday, March 11, was not obeyed. Most of the soldiers, as Buchanan had predicted months before, refused to shoot. Crowds singing the *Marseillaise* surged around the duma. The whole city was in excitement and on the streets. A soviet of the workers and soldiers of Petrograd—for "patriotic" reasons the city had Russified its original German name of St. Petersburg at the beginning of the war—was formed, and its first decision on March 14 was an order to the garrison to establish in all its units soviets of elected representatives of the lower ranks. There was an ominous paragraph in that order which frankly envisaged the establishment of a dual authority—the duma on the one hand and the soviet on the other—vesting great power in the soviets. "Orders of the military commission of the Imperial Duma," the paragraph read, "should be carried out only in those cases where they do not contradict the orders of the Soviet of Workers and Soldiers Deputies."

5. **The Revolution and the Duma.** Meanwhile the duma tried to lead the revolution into organized channels and to put itself at the head. On March 14 it appointed a Provisional Government. Its chairman was Prince George Lvov, the liberal leader of the *zemstvos,* a social reformer with a deep faith in the goodness of the common Russian people. "The newly born freedom," he declared in an interview, "will encounter great and, perhaps, exacting trials; but I face the future with confidence. I believe in the inherent strength and wisdom of our great people which has proved its greatness by the powerful thrust toward freedom that overthrew the old regime. It will prove it again by the determined whole-hearted effort to implement the principles of lib-

erty and to defend them against external and internal
enemies. It will assert the full measure of its glory, and
the rest will take care of itself." Unfortunately, Prince
Lvov, as so many of the Russian educated classes, was
wrong in his estimate of the good, common Russian man.
These good-natured romanticists adhered to the Slavophil
fallacy that the Russians were by nature democrats and
pacifists and that their rise to power would open a new
era of happiness for them and for mankind. It is hardly
astonishing that these well-meaning Russians were quickly
disappointed and that the revolution turned out entirely
differently from what they expected.

Yet at the beginning of the March Revolution the
illusion about the peaceful, glorious revolution was widespread. An American, Edward T. Heald, who was at that
time Y.M.C.A. secretary in Petrograd, wrote to his wife
a long report on the March events and closed his letter:
"It has been good to be alive these marvelous days. We
can take our hats off to the Russian people; they know
how to put great things across. Their good-nature is
impressive; even in the course of the fighting they seem
to retain their good-nature. They don't seem to have the
natures that would lead to the excesses of the French
Revolution. They handle the most exciting emergencies
in a cool matter-of-fact way. And I am struck with
their continued loyalty to the Allies. I talked with a
number of the soldiers during the week. 'Give us a week
to clean this up,' they said, 'and then we'll go back and
clean up the Germans so quick no one can stop us.' "
There could hardly have been a more pathetically wrong
prediction.

Among other prominent members of the Provisional
Government were Milyukov as Minister of Foreign Affairs and Guchkov as Minister of War. Both were determined patriots and nationalists who wished to pursue
the war on the side of the Allies until victory and to
reap for Russia the desired goal of control of the Straits
and Constantinople. The most spectacular member of
the Provisional Government, however, was a young man,
Alexander Kerensky, a lawyer and brilliant orator, then
thirty-five years old, a member of the *Trudoviki* or Labor
Party, who embodied the fire and the promise of the
revolution. His personal qualities, his position as Vice

President of the Petrograd Soviet, and his great popularity, made him at the beginning the link between the
masses and the Provisional Government in which he was
Minister of Justice. At that time, Bolshevik influence
counted for very little in the soviet. Besides Kerensky,
the Presidium of the Soviet consisted of Mensheviks.

   6. Free Russia. At the beginning, the Russian
Revolution could rightly be called "the unanimous revolution." Within five relatively bloodless days between
March 9 and March 14, Russia had been completely
transformed, at least outwardly. The old order had vanished; the new order seemed to be born under felicitous
auspices. As Kerensky put it in his memoirs which he
wrote years later and significantly called *The Crucifixion
of Liberty,* "the revolution came of its own accord, born
in the chaos of the collapse of Tsardom." The emperor
gave up autocracy without any resistance. (*See Reading
No. 21.*) He did not abdicate in favor of his son, but
of his brother Grand Duke Mikhail, who, however, declared that he would accept the throne only if invited
by a Russian Constituent Assembly which was to be
called through free elections and which was to deter-
mine the future of Russia. Thus Mikhail, too, renounced
the imperial succession, and the Russian monarchy had
reached its end, though not yet officially. No hand had
come to its help. Notwithstanding that the revolution
had been confined to Petrograd, it was immediately accepted without any active opposition throughout the
country. But lack of opposition to the revolution, it was
very soon apparent, did not mean unanimity about its
nature or Russia's future either. There was no common
language and no common purpose between the two factors trying to carry on the revolution, the duma and the
masses. The will of the masses found its theoretical expression in the soviets which were formed all over Russia and which found a common organ in the All-Russian
Congress of Soviets.
   Immediately after its creation the Provisional Government proceeded to establish complete freedom in Russia.
In 1917, for the first and so far for the last time in its
long and dolorous history, Russia was free. All existing
restrictions on the civic liberties of citizens and associa-
tions, all the inequalities under which national and re-

ligious minorities had so sorely suffered, were abolished.
Equal rights were granted to all citizens irrespective of
class, caste, race, or religion. A political amnesty was
declared and political exiles and émigrés were brought
home at the expense of the government. Even the death
penalty was abolished. Thus by the end of March, within
less than a month, Russia was a country in which democratic liberties existed, legally and actually, to a degree
hardly surpassed even in the most progressive liberal
nations. Yet the soil for such liberty was not well prepared. That liberties must go hand in hand with the
assumption of responsibilities, that they demand a sense
of fair play and consideration for the national whole,
was not realized by the masses. Liberty meant to them
the absence of authority. The lack of a tradition of self-
government was aggravated in its consequences by the
economic disorganization of the country. The situation
was not conducive to self-discipline and to constructive
action.

In this turmoil the Provisional Government faced three
difficult, complex, and urgent tasks: the convocation of
a free and democratically elected constituent assembly;
a land reform; and the conduct of foreign affairs in the
midst of a war which Russia was losing. There was general agreement on the need for the realization of the
first two tasks. But even they demanded time; the electoral law and voting procedures for the constituent assembly had to be elaborated. Finally the elections were
set for November. Land reform was in itself a complex
business and had become even more complex under the
conditions of war. Many were inclined to subject it to
detailed study and to leave its enactment to the constituent assembly. But time was running out and the masses
were eager not for careful deliberation but for quick
action. The only problem which the Provisional Government could not postpone was that of foreign policy
and the continuation of the war. On this one point, however, the duma found itself in a growing disagreement
with the people.

The Russian Revolution had been welcomed most
warmly throughout the Western world. Russia, until
then an autocracy infinitely worse than the militarist
regime in Germany, had now become a truly free coun-

try. With the impending entry of the United States into
the war, the line-up in the great struggle had by now
become ideological: on the one side were the free nations—the Western democracies and the new Russian
sister nation—on the other side were the two military
monarchies—Germany and Austria-Hungary. The liberals in the West misunderstood the Russian Revolution
and knew little of Russian history. They remembered
the French Revolution and Valmy, the heroic resistance
of the French revolutionary masses to the invaders and
their astonishing victories. Thus the Western people expected that the free Russian people would fight with a
new enthusiasm and élan for the newly won fatherland.
These hopes and illusions were shared by many educated Russians, above all, Kerensky. He tried to inspire
the war-weary army with a new offensive spirit, but the
Brusilov offensive launched in the early summer of 1917
ended after short initial successes in a complete fiasco.
Kerensky's attempts to restore discipline to the army,
"the discipline of honor and duty toward the country"
had failed.

   7. **Peace!** The truth was that the Russian army did
not wish to fight. In a dim way, without understanding
its meaning or implications, the soldiers—mostly peasants—had only one thought: peace and the return to
their farms. Some adopted the slogans of the Zimmerwald Manifesto which Lenin had drafted in 1915: "The
war which has produced this chaos is the outcome of
imperialism, of the endeavors of capitalist classes of
every nation to satisfy their greed for profit by the exploitation of human labor and the treasures of nature. . . . The task for us is the task to take up the
fight for peace, for peace without annexations or war
indemnities. . . . The right of nations to dispose of
themselves must be the immovable fundamental principle of international relations." The Russian soldiers demanded the earliest conclusion of peace without victory
on the basis of the slogan "without annexations or war
indemnities." They rejected by word, and especially by
deed, the thesis of Milyukov and Guchkov who believed
that the revolution had removed the greatest obstacle to
the war, the corrupt and inefficient tsarist government,
and that henceforth the Russian people would make all

the sacrifices necessary to achieve, together with its democratic allies, the conditions for a lasting peace through
victory. The result of this disagreement was, at the end
of April, Milyukov's and Guchkov's resignation from the
government.

8. Lenin. Their resignation led to the first recon-
struction of the Provisional Government at the beginning of May. Its new composition signified a shift to the
left, a rapprochement with the point of view represented
by the democratic socialist parties—the Mensheviks and
the Social Revolutionaries—who determined the policy
of the soviet. Meanwhile, however, on April 16, Lenin
had arrived at the Finnish railroad station in Petrograd.
His transit through Germany had been made possible by
the German General Staff who rightly expected that he
would help further disintegrate the Russian army. To
facilitate Lenin's voyage to Russia was probably a short-
sighted strategy on the part of the Germans. True, it
seemed to bring their victory over Russia and thereby
perhaps victory over the Allies nearer to realization. But
in its end effects it brought unforeseen misfortunes for
the Russian people, for Germany itself, and for the whole
West. The German General Staff obviously cared little
for the West which it regarded as its enemy. Lenin
cared even less for the West which to him was the
enemy in an even more fundamental way than the Germans. The West and its civilization represented everything that Lenin was determined to destroy. But he wished
also to uproot all Western influence in Russia. In those
days, the growing penetration of Western ideas into Russia had helped the birth of the new reign of political
liberty and democratic equality, the abolition of the traditional police regime, the confidence in the ability of
the common man to think for himself and to help decide the life of the nation. For these liberties, however,
the Russian masses cared not much more than Lenin.
His adversaries—both liberals and socialists—cared for
them, and cared for them very much. They meant to
them the fulfillment of the longings and labors of many
years. But this reliance on Western ways represented the
fundamental weakness of the liberals and socialists in
their competition with Lenin for the leadership of the
revolution.

When Lenin arrived in Petrograd he immediately demanded a relentless struggle against the Provisional Government and called for the establishment of a soviet
state, the nationalization of all land, and a mass propaganda in the army which would encourage the soldiers
to fraternize with the enemy. It is interesting to note
that the Petrograd Committee of the Bolshevik Party
rejected these proposals by an overwhelming majority.
Plekhanov, the teacher of Russian Marxism, called them
delirious. On account of his extreme radicalism, Lenin
seemed to the educated classes an impractical firebrand
and less dangerous than if he had been more "moderate"
and "realistic."

But Lenin, an accomplished master in demagogic
propaganda, knew the masses. His two simple slogans,
"End the war immediately" and "All land to the peasants," won their acclaim. The by now more outspoken
leftist character of the second Provisional Government,
in which Kerensky became Minister of War and Victor
Chernov, the leader of the Socialist Revolutionaries and
a life-long fighter for peasant aspirations, became Minister of Agriculture, did not help the situation. The soviets, too, had moved to the left. That does not mean
that they were taken over by the Bolsheviks. The First
All-Russian Congress of the Soviets which met in June
counted hardly more than one-fifth of its members as
Bolsheviks or pro-Bolshevik. The July uprising in Petrograd, which began as a demonstration by part of the
garrison against the plans of an army offensive on the
front, was taken over by the Bolshevik Party but turned
out to be a complete failure. Even the masses in Petrograd were not yet ripe for Lenin's seizure of power.
Lenin himself went into hiding in Finland. Yet the Provisional Government did not use its temporary success
for a decisive action against the Bolsheviks. It was once
more reorganized. Prince Lvov disappeared and Kerensky
became Premier and to an ever-growing degree his person and his oratory embodied the government.

9. "All Power to the Soviets." The triumph of the
Provisional Government was short-lived. General Lavr
Kornilov (1870-1918), the son of a poor peasant family,
who had distinguished himself in the war by integrity
and great courage but who had no political intelligence

or experience, planned a military coup in order to create
a strong government for the prosecution of the war. His
attempt in late summer failed. The result was a further
radicalization both of the Provisional Government which
was again reorganized and of the soviets. For the first
time, the Petrograd and the Moscow Soviets had a Bolshevik majority. The Petrograd Soviet had the advantage
of Trotsky's leadership. Though Trotsky had joined the
Bolshevik Party only in the summer of 1917, he, through
his brilliance and energy, quickly assumed second place
to Lenin. Under his leadership a workers' militia was
formed in Petrograd to protect the revolution against
counter-revolutionary attempts like that led by General
Kornilov, whose program included the abolition of the
soviets and of their position as a power equal and sometimes superior to that of the Provisional Government.
Out of this militia developed the Red Guard; a few
weeks later it staged the coup which carried Lenin to
power. In that situation, the Bolsheviks propounded the
slogan "All Power to the Soviets." This transfer of all
power to the councils of workers and soldiers implied
the end of the Provisional Government, a result dra-
matically opposed to the one which General Kornilov
had hoped to achieve.

What the Bolsheviks, and above all Lenin, wanted to
gain through their slogan, however, was not the transfer
of power to the soviets and the creation of a socialist
government responsible to the soviets and later on to
the elected constituent assembly, but the opportunity for
a successful armed insurrection in accordance with the
theories which Lenin had held for a long time. When
tactical reasons demanded it, Lenin never hesitated to
put forward false claims for his party. These claims won
most of the support the Bolsheviks had then in Russia.
"Our party alone, by taking power," Lenin grandilo-
quently informed the people, "will assure the convocation of the constituent assembly." Subsequent events
made it quite clear that Lenin had no use or consideration for a freely elected assembly. To gain other sympathies, Lenin accused the Western "capitalists" of conniving with the German imperialists, a stratagem used
again by communists and their fellow-travelers twenty
years later. Lenin hinted that there was a danger of a

separate peace between "the British and the German
imperialists" so that they might take combined action
against the Russian proletarian revolution. As in 1939,
no such negotiations for a separate peace were taking
place; on the contrary, what was to happen was the very
opposite: a separate peace was concluded between the
Bolsheviks and the German "imperialists," a peace which
in 1918, as in 1939, would allow these imperialists to
throw all their forces against the Western democracies.
The opportunity offered the Germans by the Russian-
German peace might have assured their victory in 1918
if America had not intervened.

10. Lenin's Coup d'état.   Though most members of
the Bolshevik Central Executive Committee opposed an
immediate insurrection, Lenin demanded it. By the end
of October he was convinced that the tide was carrying
the Bolsheviks to power not only in Russia but throughout the world. "The world workers' revolution has begun," he wrote on October 20. "Doubts are impossible.
We stand on the threshold of the world proletarian revolution." Lenin imposed his will upon the party and
won over large parts of the masses by assuming the role
of a spokesman for an extreme pacifism and an extreme
form of democracy. The man who more fervently than
anyone else believed in inexorable class war and in the
imposition of the absolute will of an iron dictatorship
upon the masses now promised them an almost anar-
chistic liberty and the end of all wars. "The party fights,"
Lenin wrote, "for a more democratic workers and peasants republic, in which the police and the standing army
will be completely abolished and replaced by the universally armed people, by a universal militia; all official
persons will be not only elected, but also subject to recall at any time upon the demand of a majority of the
electors; all official persons, without exception, will be
paid at a rate not exceeding the average wage of a com-
petent worker." The workers were promised free control
over industry; the peasants, free control of the land; the
country, immediate peace.

Yet even by accepting outwardly all the demands of
the masses, the Bolsheviks were in no way certain of
commanding a majority among the people. Whatever
sympathy there existed among the Russian masses for

the Bolshevik Party was not for a dictatorship which would re-introduce the autocratic police regime and impose a stricter control over workers and peasants than had existed before. But Lenin not only distrusted and disregarded the will of the people: he had no greater respect for the will of the soviets either nor any greater assurance of his ability to control the will of the soviets in freedom. Thus he decided to put the soviets before an accomplished fact. The second All-Russian Congress of Soviets was to convene on November 8, but as the outcome of a vote in this Congress was uncertain, Lenin anticipated the vote by an uprising on November 7 which put him into power. The uprising was carried through by the Military Revolutionary Committee of the Petrograd Soviet; unfortunately the moderate Socialists boycotted the Committee, a mistaken policy which left the Bolsheviks and Trotsky, who was its chairman, in complete control. Trotsky's propaganda and brilliant oratory secured the sympathy of the soldiers of the Petrograd garrison. In addition, Lenin could also rely on the support of the sailors from the Russian naval units stationed at Kronstadt, the naval base nearest to Petrograd. The counter-measures taken by the government were ineffectual and came too late.

The next day the Mensheviks and the Socialist Revolutionaries protested against Lenin's military coup and the illegal seizure of power. In a meaningless gesture of moral condemnation, they withdrew from the Congress of Soviets and thereby gave their adversaries undisputed control. The same mistake was later repeated in Italy in 1924 by the enemies of fascism in the Italian parliament and afforded Mussolini the possibility of establishing a totalitarian dictatorship after Lenin's model.

But the moderate Socialists were not alone in 1917 in protesting Lenin's coup. Leading worker organizations demanded a coalition government of all the socialist parties. Of the fifteen members of Lenin's government, which was now called Council of People's Commissars, eleven joined in a public declaration against Lenin's rule by force: "We are in favor of a socialist government composed of all the parties. We consider that only the creation of such a government can possibly guarantee the results of the heroic struggle of the working class and the revolutionary army. Outside of that, there remains only one way: the constitution of a purely Bolshevik government by means of political terror. This last is the road taken by (Lenin). We cannot and will not follow it. We see that this road leads directly to the elimination from political life of many proletarian organizations, to the establishment of an irresponsible regime, and to the destruction of the revolution." This declaration by leading socialists, among them several members of the Bolshevik Party, clearly foresaw the result of Lenin's coup.

This coup was certainly an event of tremendous importance, not only for Russia but for the world at large. A young American journalist John Reed (1887-1920) was at that time in Russia. Later he organized the Communist Labor Party in the United States. On his return to Russia he joined the party there and died in Moscow, where he was buried in the Kremlin. He described the events which culminated in Lenin's seizure of power in a book *Ten Days That Shook the World* (1919) which was widely read at that time but was later suppressed in the Soviet Union because it did not (and could not) depict Stalin's (nonexistent) leading role in the events. Instead of glorifying Stalin, Reed wrote of Trotsky's brilliant leadership. But his descriptive title was well chosen, better than most people then suspected. For in 1917-1918 the conviction was widespread, in Russia and outside Russia, that the Bolshevik government could last only a short time. Yet the government established by Lenin was to last for many decades. Though it was based on the "suicide" or the rejection of the main forces in modern Russian history, it had deep roots in much of the Russian past. To quote another well-known witness of the events of 1917, the British diplomat Sir Robert Bruce Lockhart: "The Tsar committed suicide by too much reaction. The Russian liberals and right-wing socialists committed suicide by too much freedom. Although Lenin turned society upside down, he restored to Russia the iron discipline, the secret police, the terror and the silent tongue to which she had been accustomed ever since there was a Russia."

It has become customary to call Lenin's coup the second Russian revolution of 1917. According to the Julian calendar, then still in force in Russia, the date of the coup was not the 7th of November but the 25th of October; thus it has been celebrated in the communist world as the October Revolution. To the younger generations it has so far obliterated the March Revolution of the same year (or the February Revolution according to the Julian calendar) that there has grown up a widespread belief that Lenin had overthrown tsarist autocracy and put an end to its iniquities. In reality, tsardom, with all its accompanying evils, had been overthrown by the Russian Revolution of March, 1917, which immediately introduced democratic liberty in Russia. The revolutionary tradition of 1688, of 1776, and of 1789 meant the secure establishment of the rights of man and citizen against an autocratic or arbitrary government. The revolution of March, 1917, was originally conceived in the same spirit. It was to end the long struggle for constitutional reforms which had begun in Russia in the early nineteenth century and had marked the character of modern Russia. In that sense, Lenin's coup was not a revolution but a counter-revolution. It put an end to the liberal development in Russia and reimposed a more efficient autocracy and police regime than Russia or mankind had ever known before.

11. **Lenin's Government.** This unexpected change from liberty to a ruthless dictatorship was also one of the reasons why the government created by Lenin did stay in power so much longer than it was generally believed that it could last. For Lenin established the first totalitarian government in history which had at its disposal all the modern technological means of enforcement and propaganda. Before 1917 hardly anyone could foresee the nature of such a government which ran counter to all Western traditions and all Russian hopes for freedom. Nor did the Russian people intend the creation of such a government, though the autocratic traditions of the country and the still undeveloped sense of civic responsibility and individual rights made the establishment of such a government easier in Russia than in Western countries. Yet even in Russia, Lenin's coup would have been unthinkable without the social and moral chaos created by defeat in war, economic dislocation, and governmental inefficiency.

Though the new government immediately introduced

revolutionary tribunals and "people's courts" to dispense "justice" not according to law but according to the "sense" of the people and the needs of the government— a procedure later followed by National Socialist Germany —and though "bourgeois" leaders were imprisoned or forced into hiding and non-socialist newspapers were suppressed, the elections to the constituent assembly held on November 25 gave the Bolsheviks only 175 out of 707 seats. The vast majority of the seats went to the moderate socialist parties. But under Lenin, the Constituent Assembly was doomed as all liberty in Russia was doomed. When the Assembly met on January 18, 1918, Victor Chernov was elected its chairman. Its life-span lasted only one day. As it refused to do the will of the Bolshevik minority, it was dissolved in spite of the sympathy demonstrations staged for it by Petrograd workers. Its end had more symbolic than practical significance, for several generations of educated classes in Russia had set their hopes in such a freely elected constituent assembly. But now its passing went almost unnoticed. As Professor Florinsky pointed out, the Constituent Assembly never captured the imagination of the masses; in the midst of the political, economic and social chaos that overcame Russia in the terrible winter of 1917-18—a chaos resulting from war and misgovernment but considerably aggravated by the Bolshevik seizure of power—the Constituent Assembly was almost forgotten by illiterate masses who were hardly cognizant of democratic methods and problems.

12. The Terror.   Even before the dispersal of the Constituent Assembly, the communist government—the Bolshevik Party changed its official name to Communist Party—had established on December 19, 1917, the All-Russian Extraordinary Commission to deal with the "enemies of the revolution," which meant in this case anyone whom the Bolshevik dictatorship suspected of being opposed to it. This commission, which was called *Cheka* in an abbreviated form of its Russian name, has constituted throughout the years one of the main pillars of the Bolshevik regime. It has changed its name several times, but it has never lost its character as an instrument of unrelenting and ruthless governmental terror. It was the successor to the ill-reputed security police of the

tsarist regime, the "Section III" of His Majesty's Own
Chancery, instituted in 1826 after the suppression of the
Decembrist uprising. The section, which acted against
suspicious or undesirable persons, "very often assumed
judicial functions and determined the guilt of persons in
matters which had nothing to do with public safety. . . .
There was no aspect of Russian life that would escape
its control." The government of Nicolai I was convinced
that in order to make its subjects happy, it "had to know
what was going on among the people, what were their
thoughts, what they talked about, what occupied them.
It became necessary to penetrate men's hearts and most
secret thoughts." Lenin shared the convictions of Nicolai
I. The function of the tsarist secret police which was outside and above the law was revived by Lenin and made
infinitely more efficient. As Nikita Khrushchev's speech
before the 20th Communist Party Conference of the
Soviet Union in February, 1956, brought out—or rather
confirmed what had been generally known—this regime
under the Bolshevik rule led to arbitrariness and abuses
more shocking than even those under the tsarist regime.
(*See Reading No. 23*)

Lenin made, only one was realized: the conclusion of
peace with Germany. Communist emissaries met in December, 1917, with representatives of the high command of Germany and her allies at Brest-Litovsk. The
peace treaty was signed there on March 3, 1918. Under
its terms, Russia lost all its western possessions with a
population of 52 million people. These territories were
largely inhabited by non-Russian populations and the
establishment of the new states there—Finland, Estonia,
Latvia, Lithuania, Poland, and the Ukraine—certainly
coincided with the wish of the people and the principle
of national self-determination. Neither Lithuanians nor
Ukrainians, not to mention the Finns or Poles, had any
desire to be ruled by a Russian government. But the
German government—as the communists were to do later
—used the principle of national self-determination for
its own purposes. The new states to be established were
in fact, if not in name, German protectorates or satellites.
The Germans cared little for these small peoples and
their will. What mattered to them was the fact that the
Treaty of Brest-Litobsk brought them, at least for a short

while, two great advantages: it allowed them, by abolishing the second front, to throw all their forces against the West and it promised to undo the effects of the British blockade by the wheat and coal which Germany expected to get from the Ukraine and the Donets Basin.

In the situation as it existed in the winter of 1917-18, Lenin could hardly do otherwise but conclude the peace, for Russia was—largely due to Lenin's agitation—in no condition to continue the war. But Lenin's action hardly revealed the farsightedness which his admirers claim for him. He expected the peace treaty to be only the beginning of a German, and quickly of a world, revolution. Yet Germany might easily have won the war and, in that case, undoubtedly would have turned against Russia and expanded her sphere of influence there. That this did not happen was due not to Lenin's genius but to the "capitalistic" armies of the West. When the Allies achieved victory over Germany against all the odds which the Treaty of Brest-Litovsk imposed upon them, they forced the Germans to abrogate it.

14. The Civil War. The conclusion of the peace with Germany aroused the indignation not only of the Allies but also of many patriotic elements in Russia. It led to Allied intervention in an effort to reestablish a second front in the east with the help of the Russian "patriots." But the leaders of the anti-Bolshevik armies, which were called White armies, fighting the Red army, did not inspire confidence in the masses. Among the Whites were many sincere patriots, liberals, and socialists, but among them were also too many persons who thought only of restoring the old order and whose presence recalled to the people the corruption and iniquities of the past. The Ukraine was once more turned into the scene of vast Jewish pogroms. Soon it became apparent that the Whites did not fight to support, and to carry on, the revolution, but that they were, like Lenin's regime, bent upon destroying Russia's short-lived and West-inspired liberty. Their intention was at that time more apparent and more openly acknowledged than that of Lenin; thus the masses supported either the Bolsheviks or showed themselves indifferent to the issues of the civil war. Because of the weakness of the liberal tradition in Russia, the country was faced in 1919 with that famous alternative of an exclusive choice between Red and White, between anti-liberal communism and anti-liberal reaction, an alternative which, largely due to communist and fascist propaganda, unfortunately confused Europe in the 1930's.

It was, however, not only the obvious and glaring insufficiency of the Whites to represent liberty and the revolution against the Reds which lost them the civil war. There was much vehement discord in the ranks of the adversaries of the communists and also between them and the Western powers who had hoped for the emergence not of a reactionary but of a liberal Russia. This confusion and disunity contrasted with the strict unity of purpose and leadership which prevailed in the communist ranks and in the Red army under Trotsky. The communists were also helped by their willing promises at that time to fulfill the two most important demands of the people: land to the peasants and independence to the national minorities. National independence, or at least real autonomy, for the many subject nationalities of the Russian empire was an especially urgent problem in the territories which formed the basis of the White armies. The Bolsheviks originally held the center of the Russian empire around Moscow, inhabited only by Russians, and thus did not have to meet the problem of independence for the non-Russian peoples immediately. They were most generous in promising full national self-determination, expecting to be free later to interpret it as they saw fit.

On the other hand, the Whites, who gathered their forces in the outlying provinces of the empire where non-Russian peoples predominated, made no secret of their intention to restore the unity of the Russian empire and of denying the rights of self-determination to its subject nationalities. Among the officers and leading spokesmen of the White armies were many landowners in whose presence and activities the peasants, not without justification, saw the threat of again being deprived of the lands which they had meanwhile appropriated. The fate of the White armies was sealed when, after their victory over the Germans, the Allies lost interest in reestablishing an eastern front and in supporting the White armies.

The Allied refusal of energetic action in Russia was

motivated by a not unusual combination of disillusion
with the Whites, war-weariness, and wishful thinking.
Thus both the Allied intervention and the White resistance collapsed in 1919 and by 1920 the communists
were in full control of Russia. The civil war, which later
was regarded as the heroic stage of the communist conquest of power over the vast empire, was ended. Russia
entered, after a brief promise of a brighter future, a
new stage in its long history of sorrow and oppression.

15. Russia under the Communist Regime. Victory
in the civil war entrenched Lenin and his party in power.
Like the National Socialists in Germany fifteen years
later, the communists took good care to destroy all
organized opposition and to remove, through the dread
of terror, the possibility of its revival. As the heirs of a
long tradition of conspiratorial activity they could master-
mind their secret police better than the tsarist government had been able to do. Once in power, the Bolsheviks
could also easily forget most of their promises. Their
regime in many respects turned out much differently from
what most people had expected. The state did not wither
away but became more powerful and all-pervasive than
any state had ever been. The Soviets, to whom the dema-
goguery of Lenin wished to give all power, lost all the
power which they had exercised under the Provisional
Government; they became a negligible rubber-stamp for
the decisions of the party leadership. They lived only in
the official name of soviet government.

The peasants lost the ownership and control of the land
which they thought was their own in 1919 and for which
they had longed for such a long time. Now they were put
under strict bureaucratic control; heavy deliveries of
grain and foodstuffs to the authorities were enforced;
as in former times but to an increased degree, the peasantry bore the excessive burden of the industrialization
and militarization of the country. In all the fertile lands
under the communist regime, agrarian production was
unable to assure a decent standard of living for the population. The insensate rate of industrialization strengthened
the armed forces but did not increase the supply of consumer goods. The workers did not control the factories
or working conditions but were overworked in the interests of the state monopoly.

Millions of people died from starvation, forced hard labor, or mass migrations. Whenever a country fell under communist domination, this process repeated itself. The impoverishment was not confined to material goods; Russia's intellectual and cultural life was put into a strait jacket of dogmatic authoritarianism which did not allow free creative expression. The endless discussion of Marxist-Leninist doctrine enveloped all intellectual life with a blight of boredom. In all these aspects, conditions in Russia did not improve but grew worse as time progressed and as the regime became more firmly established.

The industrialization of Russia in recent decades has been hailed as a great achievement. But it should not be forgotten that in 1914 Russia possessed the foundations of a modern industrial system, of Western scholarship and technical skill, and that Japan, with infinitely less resources and without any modern foundation, achieved before the First World War a similar industrialization and a rapid decline in illiteracy without the human depredations which accompanied this process in communist Russia. Yet in spite of its shortcomings and cruelties, the rapid industrialization of Russia released much popular energy and gave the people a sense of purposefulness.

Against the internationalist expectations voiced in 1917-1919, the communist regime showed its greatest attractiveness to the Russian people by unexpectedly enhancing Russian nationalist pride and by securing for Russia a position of greater power than the most powerful tsars achieved. With the rapid build-up of heavy armaments and giant industrial combines, the stagnancy characteristic of nineteenth-century Russian economic and social life was broken. The image of the "superfluous man" lost its significance. Even subject nationalities received in the beginning much encouragement in their cultural life and promises of a fuller participation in economic advance. New symbols were introduced to give them the feeling of equality with the Russians, and the right to use and develop their languages, which had been suppressed under the tsarist regime, was not only recognized but actively promoted.

These considerable initial gains for the subject peoples were, however, largely annulled in the 1930's and the

various nationalities were not only subjected—as the
Great Russians were themselves—to the deadening uni-
formity of an intellectual and political autocracy, but
the leading role of the Great Russian people among the
peoples of the Union of Soviet Socialist Republics—as
the Russian empire was renamed—and the obligation of
these peoples to accept gratefully this leadership were
reemphasized.

16. Communism as a Creed. Communism—the
Leninist interpretation of Marxism—has been raised in
Russia to the rank of an official religion of the state. The
communist state represented by the party leadership has
become identical with the communist "church," and thus
claims to be, to an unprecedented degree, the guide and
embodiment of all forms and activities of life, the supreme arbiter of what is good and evil. To an unprecedented degree, too, the communist state was able to en-
force this claim. Its creed was a hard, jealous, and exces-
sively dogmatic "religion" which tried to monopolize all
of man's loyalties to the exclusion even of his loyalty to
family or friends. The creed explained all shortcomings,
all the glaring discrepancies between theory and reality,
by the existence and activity of devilish forces at home
and abroad, enemies of the people or of the revolution,
saboteurs and warmongers who by their ever-present
menace forced communism into militant vigilance.

Communism was a religion without charity or mercy,
filled with implacable hatred, and convinced that all of
right and the whole future were always on its side. Total
commitment to permanent struggle was demanded from
all its adherents. Their "religious" fervor was strengthened by the presentation of all situations as clear-cut
either-or choices for which the party, with its "scientific"
understanding of history, always had the right answer.
The inevitable triumph of communism, thanks to the infallible leadership of its hierarchy, it was predicted, would
assure for mankind a perfect social order and the end
of all troubles on earth. Among the faithful—and among
the noncritical and often spellbound admirers—it was
overlooked how often the leadership, beginning with
Lenin, had been wrong.

The realization of Lenin's expectations of the doom
of capitalist society and of the imminent triumph of com-

munist world revolution seems today, forty years after
his seizure of power, more remote than they did during
his lifetime. Yet at the Sixth Congress of Soviets which
met in Moscow on November 6, 1918, Lenin declared:
"A complete victory of the socialist revolution is unthinkable in any one country. It requires at least the cooperation of several advanced countries, and Russia is not
one of them. This is why the question as to the expansion of the revolution into other lands . . . becomes one
of the principal problems of the Revolution. . . . We
must raise the proletariat of all countries. . . . We can
see already how the fire has broken out in most countries
—in America, in Germany, in England." Lenin was then
convinced that "the peace which the rapacious imperialists of England and France are going to inflict on conquered Europe" will arouse the proletarian revolution
throughout Europe. "They are raising a Chinese wall
against Bolshevism (in Europe), but Bolshevism will
pass the wall and spread its infection among the willing
men of all countries." In accordance with Lenin, Jacob
Sverdlov, one of his closest collaborators in 1917-18,
President of the Executive Committee of the Congress of
Soviets and Stalin's predecessor as Secretary of the Communist Party, declared in 1918 that within six months
Soviet rule would be triumphant not only in Hungary
(where a short-lived communist regime was then in
power) but in Austria and Germany, in France and
Great Britain.

It is hardly astonishing that Lenin and his successors
misunderstood the outside world and the nature of Western society. They beclouded reality by their dogmatic
application of Marxist concepts to it. Marx's interpretation of capitalism, which described the situation in the
Western industrialized countries of the 1850's, had nothing in common with the reality there in the 1950's. In
the century since Marx, Western society has shown a
dynamic vitality which has enabled it to integrate labor
fully into its political, social, and cultural texture and to
allow it to share in the benefits of a rapidly expanding
economy. Modern Western life has proven itself a truly
permanent revolution, an unbroken search for greater
freedom and higher standards of living. Communism, in
its Leninist form, has had no attraction for the West.

17. Russia and World Revolution. Lenin was partly right, however, in the point where he fundamentally diverged from Marx who pinned his hope for communism on the workers in the most highly developed countries. Lenin took a different view because, in spite of all his Marxism, he was deeply steeped in Russian traditions and conditions. Though Lenin claimed to be a disciple of Marx, he was equally indebted to the Russian revolutionary tradition, especially to Tkachev and Bakunin, an indebtedness of which he was hardly aware because this legacy was part and parcel of the atmosphere in which he grew up. Bakunin's anarchism represented, to quote Dr. Eugene Pyziur, the most recent student of Bakuninism, a strange amalgam of utopian rules for the securing of total liberty and very much non-utopian ones for the conquest of political power and the establishment of the most severe social discipline. Any attempt to put Bakunin's theories into practice would naturally not be able to realize its utopian elements of liberty and thus leave its rather savage disciplinary element without any counter-balance by mitigating factors. The result would be a total despotism as it came about when Lenin, after having written his utopian *The State and the Revolution* on the eve of his coup, seized power a short while later.

Bakunin's principles, with their insistence on a disciplined conspiracy rigidly united in theory and action, unleashing the revolutionary instincts of the masses, and on the closest cooperation between the peasants and urban workers, were worked out for the particular Russian conditions. In 1917 the conditions for revolution which Bakunin postulated were present, and the result which he anticipated in such a situation came about. The techniques of the Bolshevik revolution were those proposed by Bakunin. "Marxism only provided a more attractive label and more reasonable goals behind which the essence of Bolshevism might hide itself more easily." Like Bakunin, Lenin not only rejected Western democratic methods for which he had no understanding, but grasped the revolutionary importance of dissatisfied and backward peasants as no European socialist could. But the student must be warned against assuming that the Bolshevik coup of November, 1917, was the logical or necessary outcome of modern Russian history. On the contrary, it was, to a very large extent, its denial and reversal. During its modern period, Russia had become politically, economically, and culturally more and more a part of Europe. This process was well on its way in 1917, but it was far from being completed. It was this incompletion which made Lenin's coup possible. (*See Reading No. 22.*)

Lenin saw Western society and civilization as the great enemy. He expected that Russia would develop a new society and civilization, infinitely superior to, and finally triumphant over, the West. Therein he shared some of the most chimerical expectations of the extreme Slavophils. He went even further than they did. For he not only turned Russia against the West, but looked toward Asia to support Russia in the struggle against the West and to assure Russia's victory in this globe-encompassing conflict. Lenin was the first Marxist to understand the significance of the revolutionary nationalist movements of Asia and Africa for the overthrow of Western and capitalist world leadership. He anticipated the irrepressible dynamism of the by then only incipient Afro-Asian nationalism in arousing the masses.

As early as at the Bolshevik conference of January, 1912, Lenin greeted the Chinese nationalists and declared that the Chinese revolution of that year was "from our point of view an event of world importance toward achieving the liberation of Asia and the overthrow of European mastery." As soon as Lenin came to power he planned for the unity, as he called it, of the Russian proletarian revolution and the Asian nationalist revolutions in a common effort to destroy the West. Shortly before his death he expressed his conviction that "the outcome of the struggle for the control of the world depends on the fact that Russia, India, China, etc., contain the vast majority of the world's population. This majority has progressed more rapidly every year on the road to freedom and in this sense there can be no shadow of a doubt as to the final outcome of the world struggle."

With Lenin's seizure of power a period of Russian history had come to an end, the period which might be called modern Russia. It was almost a symbolic act when Lenin transferred the capital of the Russian empire from St. Petersburg back to Moscow in March, 1918. Con-

temporary Russian history, again dominated by Moscow
in a more absolute fashion than even under the Muscovite princes who ruled from the Kremlin in the fifteenth
and sixteenth centuries, resembles in many ways that
earlier period.

Yet Russian history goes on, and forces of Western
liberty which Lenin sought to suppress may one day be
reawakened. In 1957 fewer people will be convinced
that Russia's modern history has come definitely to an
end than there might have been in 1947. The events of
1956 and 1957 have gone far to show that even communist totalitarian indoctrination has been unable to suppress the spirit of liberty in communist-dominated lands.
When the iron curtain which the communists drew
around these lands to preserve them from any contact
with the outside world was only slightly lifted, it was
sufficient—as it had been in the eighteenth and early
nineteenth centuries—to awake in the unfortunate peoples under communist domination the desire not only for
a betterment of their living conditions but for the freedom of creative and intellectual expression. Forty years
after Lenin's coup, Russia and the countries under its
domination suffered not only from a severe economic
crisis, but the communist party itself was in the midst of
an ideological crisis which put many of the dogmas held
unshakable in 1947 to a severe test.

There is still good hope for Russia and the Russian
people—that they may one day resume the course of
their modern history and reenter the full partnership with
Europe to which so many Russians aspired at the beginning of the twentieth century.

Part II

SELECTED READINGS

— Reading No. 1 —

COXE: *RUSSIA IN 1790*[1]

William Coxe (1747-1828), an Englishman, traveled in Northern and Eastern Europe at the end of the eighteenth century. In Book V of his widely read report on his travels he described the conditions which he found in Russia.

↑   ↑   ↑

Much has been written concerning the great civilization which Peter I, introduced into this country; that he obliged the peoples to relinquish their beards, and their national dress; that he naturalized the arts and sciences; that he disciplined his army, and created a navy; and that he made a total change throughout each part of his extensive empire. We may readily allow the truth of this eulogium with respect to his improvements in the discipline of his army and the creation of a navy; for these were objects within the reach of the persevering genius of a despotic sovereign: but the pompous accounts of the total change which he effected in the national manners, seem to have been the mere echoes of foreigners, who have never visited the country, and who have collected the history of Peter from the most partial information. For though a nation, when compared with itself at a former period, may have made a rapid progress towards improvement, even when the degree of that improvement, if put in competition with the refinements of other nations, seems scarcely to exist; yet as the exaggerated accounts which I had heard and read of the great civilization diffused throughout the whole empire, made me expect a more polished state of manners than I found; I must own I was astonished at the barbarism in which the bulk of the people still continue. I am ready to allow that the principal nobles

[1] From William Coxe, *Travels into Poland, Russia, Sweden and Denmark,* 5 vols., vol. III, 4th ed. (London: T. Cadell, 1792), pp. 152, 162.

are as civilized, and as refined in their entertainment, mode of living, and social intercourse, as those of other European countries. But there is a wide difference between polishing a nation, and polishing a few individuals. The merchants and peasants still universally retain their beards, their national dress, their original manners; and, what is most remarkable, the greatest part of the merchants and burghers of the large towns, even the citizens of Petersburgh and Moscow, resemble, in their external appearance and general mode of living, the inhabitants of the smallest village. . . .

The greatest part of the peasants, who form the bulk of the nation, are still almost as deficient in the arts as they were before Peter's time, although the sciences have flourished in the capital. But the civilization of a numerous and widely dispersed people cannot be the work of a moment; and can only be effected by a gradual and almost insensible progress. . . .

The parochial clergy, who may and ought to be the most useful members of society, are generally, in Russia, the very refuse of the people. It is literally true, that many of them cannot even read, in their own language, the Gospel which they are commissioned to preach. . . . Nor is it in the least surprising that some are so illiterate, when we consider the scanty maintenance which they derive from their profession. Besides the surplice fees, which in the poorest benefices amount to £.4 per annum, and in the most profitable to about £.20; they have only a wooden house, scarcely superiour to that of the meanest among their parishioners and a small portion of land, which they usually cultivate with their own hands. While the highest dignity to which they can ever attain, as long as they continue married, is that of protopope of a cathedral, whose income scarcely exceeds £.20 a year. As the parish priests are undoubtedly the principal sources from which learning and improvement must generally be diffused among the poorer class of people; if they, who ought to instruct and enlighten others, are so ignorant, how gross must be the ignorance of their parishioners! . . . .

CLARKE: *RUSSIAN NOBILITY IN 1800*[2]

Edward Daniel Clarke (1769-1822), an English scientist, made an extended tour of Europe, Egypt, and Palestine in the years from 1799 to 1803. His description tells us how Europeans looked upon Russian nobility at the beginning of the nineteenth century.

✓   ✓   ✓

The Russian nobility are passionately fond of travelling, . . . They entertain extravagant notions of the wealth and happiness of Englishmen; and they have good reason to do so, since whatever they possess useful or estimable comes to them from England. Books, maps, prints, furniture, clothing, hardware, of all kinds, horses, carriages; hats, leather, medicine, almost every article of convenience, comfort or luxury, must be derived from England, or it is of no estimation. Some of the nobles are much richer than the richest of our English peers; and a vast number, as may be supposed, are very poor. To this poverty, and to these riches, are equally joined the most abject manners and the most detestable profligacy. In sensuality, they are without limits of law, conscience, or honour. In their amusement, always children; the toys of infants, the baubles of French fops, constitute the highest object of their wishes. Novelty delights the human race; but no part of it seek for novelty so early as the Russian nobles. Novelty in their debaucheries; novelty in gluttony; novelty in cruelty; novelty in whatever they pursue. This is not the case of the lower class, who preserve their habits unaltered from one generation to another. But there are characteristics in which the Russian prince and the Russian peasant are the same. They are all equally

[2] From Edward Daniel Clarke, *Travels in Various Countries of Europe, Asia and Africa,* Part I: Russia, Tartary, and Turkey (New York: Fay & Co., 1813), pp. 57 ff.

barbarous. Visit a Russian, of whatever rank, at his country
seat, and you will find him lounging about, uncombed,
unwashed, unshaven, half naked, eating raw turnips and
drinking kvass. The raw turnip is handed about in slices,
in the first houses, upon a silver salver, with brandy, as a
whit before dinner. Their hair is universally in a state not
to be described; and their bodies are only divested of
vermin when they frequent the bath. Upon those occasions, their shirts and pelisses are held over a hot stove,
and the heat occasions the vermin to fall off. It is a fact
too notorious to admit dispute, that from the emperor
to the meanest slave, throughout the vast empire of all
the Russians, including all its princes, nobles, priests, and
peasants, there exists not a single individual in a thousand
whose body is destitute of vermin. An English gentleman
of Moscow, residing as a banker in the city, assured me,
that passing on horseback through the streets he has often
seen women of the highest quality, sitting in the windows
of their palaces, divesting each other of vermin. . . .

The true manners of the people are not seen in Petersburgh, not even in Moscow, by entering the houses of the
nobility alone. Some of them, and generally those to whom
letters of recommendation are obtained, have travelled,
and introduced refinements, which their friends and com-
panions readily imitate. The real Russian rises at an early
hour, and breakfasts on a dram with black bread. His
dinner at noon consists of the coarsest and most greasy
viands, the effects of which are counteracted by salted
cucumbers, sour cabbage, the juices of his *vaccinium,* and
his nectar kvass. Sleep, which renders him unmindful of
his abject servitude and barbarous life, he particularly in-
dulges; sleeping always after eating, and going early to
his bed. The principal articles of diet are the same everywhere; grease and brandy. A stranger, dining with their
most refined and most accomplished princes, may in vain
expect to see his knife and fork changed. If he sends them
away, they are returned without even being wiped. If he
looks behind him, he will see a servant spit in the plate
he is to receive, and wipe it with a dirty napkin, to remove
the dust. If he ventures (which he should avoid, if he is
hungry) to inspect the soup in his plate with too inquisi-
ive an eye, he will doubtless discover living victims in
distress, which a Russian, if he saw, would swallow with

indifference. . . . But vermin unknown to an Englishman, and which it is not permitted even to name, attack the stranger who incautiously approaches too near the persons of the nobility and visit him from their sophas and chairs. If at a table he regards his neighbour, he sees him picking his teeth with his fork, and then plunging it into a plate of meat which is brought round to all. The horrors of a Russian kitchen are inconceivable and there is not a bed in the whole empire, which an English traveller, aware of the condition, would venture to approach.

. . . The generation has not yet passed away, which, at the pleasure of the Tsar, were sent to be whipped as dogs. The short liberty they enjoyed in the reign of Catherine did not suffice to elevate their minds from the depravity always incident to a state of slavery. Under Paul, the period came again in which they suffered the indignities offered to their forefathers. Potemkin, one of the meanest and most profligate of men, frequently taught them to remember what they had before been, by chastising with his own hand a prince or a nobleman with whom he chanced to be offended, and the emperor Paul exercised his cane upon the nobles who were his officers. Under such government, if we find them servile, oppressive, cowardly and tyrannical, it is no more than may be expected, from their mode of education, and the discipline they undergo. They will naturally crouch with their heads in the dust before an emperor or his favorite, and trample their inferiors beneath their feet.

It is very true, that the system of slavery in Russia, like many other evils, may sometimes be productive of good. If the nobleman is benevolent, his slaves are happy, for they are fed, clothed and lodged. In sickness they are attended, and in old age they find an asylum. In case of accidents from fire, if a whole village is burned, the nobleman must find wood to rebuild it. But when, as generally happens, the proprietor is a man without feeling or principle, their situation is indeed wretched. In such instances, the peasants often take the law into their own hands, and assassinate their lords. To prevent this, the latter live in cities, remote from their own people, and altogether unmindful of all that concerns them, except the hard tribute they are to receive. . . .

— Reading No. 3 —

ALEXANDER: *PROCLAMATION OF 1812*[3]

At the start of the Great Patriotic War of 1812 Tsar Alexander I issued the following proclamation to the Russian people.

To the Nation. The enemy has passed the frontiers, and carried the arms into the interior of Russia. Since perfidy cannot destroy an empire which has existed with a dignity always increasing for so many generations, he has determined to attack it by violence, and to assault the empire of the Czars with the forces of the continent of Europe.

With treason in the heart and loyalty on the lips, he flatters the ears of the credulous and enchains their arms; and if the captive perceives fetters under the flowers, the spirit of domination discovers itself; and he calls forth war to assure the work of treason! But Russia has penetrated his views. The path of loyalty is open to her: she has invoked the protection of God; she opposes to the plots of her enemy an army strong in courage, and eager to drive from her territory this race of locusts who consume the earth, and whom the earth will reject, finding them too heavy a burden to sustain.

We call our sufficient armies to annihilate the enemy. Our soldiers who are under arms are like lions who dart on their prey; but we do not disguise from our faithful subjects that the intrepid courage of our warriors actually ought to be proportioned to the object; and the object

[3] From General Sir Robert Wilson (1777-1849), *Narrative of Events during the Invasion of Russia by Napoleon Bonaparte and the Retreat of the French Army, 1812,* ed. by Herbert Randolph, 2nd ed. (London: J. Murray, 1866), p. 46 *f.*

placed before you is to overthrow the tyrant who wishes to overthrow all the earth.

We have called on our ancient city of Moscow, the first capital of our empire, to make final efforts, and she is accustomed to make them, by sending her sons to the succour of the empire. After her, we call on all our subjects of Europe and Asia to unite themselves for the cause of humanity! We call on all our civil and religious communities to cooperate with us by a general rising against the universal tyrant.

Whenever in this empire he turns his steps he will be assured of finding our native subjects laughing at his frauds, scorning his flattery and his falsehoods, trampling on his gold with the indignation of offended virtue, and paralyzing by the feeling of true honour, his legions of slaves. In every noble Russian he will find a Pojarskoi, in every ecclesiastic a Palistyn, in every peasant a Minin.

Nobles! you have been in all ages the defenders of our country! Holy Synod! and you members of your Church! you have in all circumstances by your intercession called down upon our empire the Divine protection! Russian people! intrepid posterity of Slavonians! it is not the first time that you have plucked out the teeth from the head of the lion, who sprung on you as upon a prey, and met his own destruction! Unite yourselves! carry the cross in your hearts and the sword in your hands, and human force never can prevail against you.

I have delegated the organization of the new levies to the nobles of every province; and I have charged with the care of assembling the brave patriots who will present themselves of their own accord for the defense of the country the gentlemen amongst whom the officers will be chosen. The number of those who will be assembled ought to be sent to Moscow, where they will be made acquainted with the commander-in-chief.

Given at our camp of Polotzk, the 18th of July, 1812.

— Reading No. 4 —

CHAADAYEV: *PETER'S LEGACY*[4]

Peter Chaadayev (1794-1856) was one of Russia's early original thinkers. He favored the Westernization of Russia and opposed the Slavophils. In 1837 he wrote the following about the role of Peter the Great in Russian history.

For three hundred years Russia has aspired to consort with Occidental Europe; for three hundred years she has taken her most serious ideas, her most fruitful teachings, and her most vivid delights from there. For over a century Russia has done better than that. One hundred and fifty years ago the greatest of our kings—the one who supposedly began a new era, and to whom, it is said, we owe our greatness, our glory, and all the goods which we own today—disavowed the old Russia in the face of the whole world. He swept away all our institutions with his powerful breath; he dug an abyss between our past and our present, and into it he threw pell-mell all our traditions. He himself went to the Occidental countries and made himself the smallest of men, and he came back to us so much the greater; he prostrated himself before the Occident, and he arose as our master and our ruler; he called his new capital by an Occidental name; he rejected his hereditary title and took an Occidental title; finally, he almost gave us his own name, and more than once he signed his sovereign decrees with an Occidental name. . . .

Do you not believe that if he had found in his country a rich and fertile history, living traditions, and deep-rooted institutions, he would have hesitated to put them into a new mold? Do you not believe that faced with a strongly

[4] From Hans Kohn, *The Mind of Modern Russia* (New Brunswick, N.J.: Rutgers University Press, 1955), pp. 50 *f.*, 53 *f.*, 55 *f.*

outlined and pronounced nationality, his founding spirit would have demanded that the nationality itself become the necessary instrument for the regeneration of his country? On the other hand, would the country have suffered being robbed of its past and a new one, a European one, being put in its place? But that was not the case. Peter the Great found only a blank page when he came to power, and with a strong hand he wrote on it the words Europe and Occident: from that time on we were part of Europe and of the Occident.

Don't be mistaken about it: no matter how enormous the genius of this man and the energy of his will, his work was possible only in the heart of a nation whose past history did not imperiously lay down the road it had to follow, whose traditions did not have the power to create its future, whose memories could be erased with impunity by an audacious legislator. We were so obedient to the voice of a prince who led us to a new life because our previous existence apparently did not give us any legitimate grounds for resistance. The most marked trait of our historical physiognomy is the absence of spontaneity in our social development. Look carefully, and you will see that each important fact in our history is a fact that was forced on us: almost every new idea is an imported idea. But there is nothing in this point of view which should give offense to the national sentiment: it is a truth and has to be accepted. . . .

But here comes another new school [the Slavophil school of thought]. It no longer wants the Occident: it wants to destroy the work of Peter the Great and again follow the desert road. Forgetting what the Occident has done for us, ungrateful towards the great man who civilized us, towards the Europe which taught us, this school repudiates both Europe and the great man; and in its hasty ardor, this newborn patriotism already proclaims that we are the cherished children of the Orient. Why, it asks, do we have to look for lights among the peoples of the Occident? Don't we have in our midst the germs of an infinitely better social order than Europe has? Why don't we leave it to time? Left to ourselves, to our lucid reason, to the fertile principle which is hidden in the depth of our powerful nature, and above all to our saintly religion, we shall soon go beyond those peoples who are a prey to errors and to lies. For what should we envy the Occident? Its religious wars, its Pope, its chivalry, its Inquisition? Truly beautiful things! Is the Occident the native land of science and of all deep things? It is the Orient, as is well known. Let us then withdraw to the Orient, which we touch everywhere and from which erstwhile we derived our beliefs, our laws, and our virtues, all that made us the most powerful people in the world. The old Orient is fading away: well, aren't we its natural heirs? Henceforth it is among us that these wonderful traditions will perpetuate themselves, that all these great and mysterious truths, with whose safekeeping we were entrusted from the very beginning, will realize themselves.

— Reading No. 5 —

GOGOL: *RUSSIA'S MISSION*[5]

In a famous passage at the end of his novel Dead Souls *(1842) Nikolai Gogol (1809-1852) compared Russia with a troika, a small sleigh drawn by three fast horses abreast, rushing over the hard crystalline snow covering the endless plains, toward Russia's goal of world leadership.*

✓   ✓   ✓

Ah, Russia, from my beautiful home in a strange land I still can see you! In you everything is poor and disordered and homely. . . . Yet what secret, what invisible force draws me to you? . . . What is it that your boundless expanses presage?

Do they not presage that one day there will arise in

[5] The most recent translation of *Dead Souls* is by George Reavey in *The Novel Library* (New York: Pantheon Books, 1948).

you ideas as boundless as yourself? Do they not presage
that one day you, too, will know no limits? Do they not
presage that one day, when again you shall have room for
daring exploits, there will spring to life the heroes of old?
. . . Yes, each time that there arises in Russia a movement of thought, it becomes clear that such a movement
sinks deep into the Slavonic nature while it would have but
skimmed the surface of other nations. . . .

Russia of mine, are you not also speeding like a troika
which nothing can overtake? Is not the road smoking beneath your wheels, and are not the bridges thundering as
you cross them, everything left behind, while the specta-
tors, struck with the portent, stop to wonder whether you
be not a thunderbolt launched from heaven? What does
that awe-inspiring progress of yours foretell? What is the
unknown force which lies within your mysterious steeds?

Surely the winds themselves must abide in their manes,
and every vein in their bodies must be an ear stretched
to catch the celestial message which bids them, with iron-
girded breasts, and hoofs which barely touch the earth as
they gallop, fly forward on a mission of God?

Whither are you speeding, Russia of mine? Whither?
Answer me! But no answer comes—only the weird sound
of your collar-bells. Rent into a thousand shreds, the air
roars past you, as you are overtaking the whole world, and
shall one day force all nations, all empires to stand aside,
to give way to you!

— Reading No. 6 —

HERZEN: *LIBERTY IN RUSSIA*[6]

*Alexander Herzen (1812-1870) was one of the few
Russian liberals in the middle of the nineteenth century.*

[6] From Hans Kohn, *The Mind of Modern Russia* (New Brunswick, N.J.: Rutgers University Press, 1955), pp. 159 *f.*,
163.

He left Russia for Europe in 1847 but was bitterly disappointed by the failure of the European revolutions of 1848. In 1851 he wrote in French his On the Development of Revolutionary Ideas in Russia.

✓   ✓   ✓

If it is horrible to live in Russia, it is as horrible to live in Europe. Why did I leave Russia? To answer this question, I shall quote some words of the farewell letter to my (Russian) friends: "Don't be mistaken! I have found here neither joy nor rest. I can't even imagine anybody finding rest or joy in Europe today. Sadness breathed in every word of my letters. Life here is very painful. I believe in nothing but the movement; I regret nothing but the victims; I love only the persecuted, I esteem only the tortured, and yet I stay. I stay to suffer twice: our own pain and that which I find here, perhaps to sink in the general dissolution. But I stay because here the struggle is wide open, because here it has a voice. Woe to the defeated here! But here he dos not succumb without making his voice heard and without having tried his strength in the struggle. For the sake of this voice, for the sake of this open struggle, for the sake of this publicity, I say!" This I wrote on March 1, 1849. . . . But if in Europe also they succeed in gagging us and if oppression no longer permits us to curse our oppressors openly, then we shall leave for America, sacrificing everything to the dignity of man and to the freedom of expression. . . .

One thought only united the Petersburg period of Russian history with that of Moscow, the thought of the aggrandizement of the state. Everything was sacrificed to it, the dignity of the rulers, the blood of the subjects, justice towards one's neighbors, and the welfare of the whole country. . . .

This discontent of which we speak cannot be easily seen. Russia always seems so tranquil that one has difficulty in believing that something is happening there. Few people know what happens beneath the shroud with which the government covers the corpses, the stains of blood, the military executions, while maintaining hypocritically and arrogantly that there is neither blood nor corpse beneath the shroud. . . .

Can one really believe that servitude, passive obedience,

and a despotic government can develop the abilities of the
Russian people? A long servitude cannot be an accident,
it must correspond to some national trait. This trait can
be absorbed and overcome by other traits, but it can also
remain victorious; if Russia accommodates herself to the
existing order, she will not have the future which we wish
for her. If she continues the period of St. Petersburg, or
if she returns to the period of Moscow, she will have no
future but to throw herself upon Europe, like a semibar-
barian and semicorrupted horde devastating the civilized
countries and perishing in the midst of general destruction. Was it not necessary therefore to call upon the Russian people to recognize its tragic conditions? . . . Instead, the Slavophils preached submission. . . . They
preached the contempt of the West, and yet the West
alone could enlighten the dark gulf of Russian life; they
glorified the past, instead of emphasizing the need of liberation from this past in favor of a future common to Russia and the West. . . .

One has remarked that an opposition which leads a
frontal attack upon a government always has itself, in an
inverted sense, something of the character of the government attacked. I believe that there is some justification
for the fear of communism which the Russian government
begins to feel: Communism is the Russian autocracy
turned upside down. . . .

— Reading No. 7 —

HERZEN: *PATRIOTISM AND SLAVES*[7]

*At the time of the Crimean War, Alexander Herzen,
who was then living in London, sent a letter to the London*
Daily News, *entitled "Conversations with the Russian*

[7] From the London *Daily News* of October 28, 1854.

Prisoners at Plymouth." The letter was printed on October 28, 1854, and was signed "A Cosmopolitan Traveler."

SIR:—It has repeatedly been said that the war of the Western Powers in favour of Turkey is not a war against a Nation, but a war against the turbulent and ill-regulated ambition of a single individual. My experience of Russia and a long study of the character of the Emperor Nicholas, carried on at St. Petersburg, have given me every reason to believe in the truth of this assertion. Nevertheless, liking to submit even my best founded convictions to such tests as may serve to strengthen or to weaken them, I thought that a visit to the Russian prisoners taken at Bomarsund might afford a curious opportunity of the kind. . . .

Will it be believed? The only fear which these unhappy men entertain, is to be obliged to return to their former life. Their captivity under the English flag they look upon as a deliverance. . . .

"I hope, my friends," said I to them, "that none of you will be obliged to resume your chains against your inclination. There is a question of sending you to Australia, should you desire it; there you will be free, as you have never been." This project, however, I am bound to confess it, did not at all seem to the taste of my auditors . . . "What should we do?" said one of the most intelligent among them to me. "What should we do in a strange and distant country, we who are unable to perform any kind of pacific work? Why do not the English and French rather enrol us among their troops?" "Is it possible," I observed, in reply, "you would fight against the Emperor Nicholas, your Sovereign?"

"He would no longer be our Sovereign, and his quarrel would no longer be ours."

These words, which I have repeated literally, proved to me what I have always thought, that we must not expect to find feelings of patriotism in the hearts of slaves. "Holy Russia"—this metaphor, which the cabinet of St. Petersburg holds out to Europe as a threat, falls like an empty sound on the ear of the enrolled Serf, and does not penetrate to the depths of his heart. To him Russia is not more "holy" than America is "free" to the plantation Negroes.

— Reading No. 8 —

RUSSIA AND THE UNITED STATES[8]

In 1866, pursuant to a resolution of Congress, an American mission under the leadership of Gustavus Vasa Fox was sent to Russia to congratulate the people on the escape of Alexander II from assassination. One of the secretaries accompanying Fox was Joseph Florimond, Duc de Loubet (1831-1927), who reported speeches delivered at a banquet given in Moscow for the American visitors.

✦　　　　✦　　　　✦

Mr. Pogodine: As an old Muscovite, thoroughly Russian, one whose life has been entirely devoted to history, I ask the president to permit me to address a few words to our dear and honorable guests. Russia and America are near to each other in spite of the enormous distance between them. It is, as we say in Russia, 'to be reached with the hand.' The telegraph has accelerated our communication, but there is another more rapid than the electric; there is another tie stronger than any metal or any diplomatic art, a tie that is expressed by our common saying, 'The heart understands the heart.' By a kind of instinct, by a second sight, like that we read of in Scott, we Russians and Americans have great consideration for each other, are equal in reciprocal love, and wish well to each other, without any other thought, not being able to explain even the reason of our mutual sincerity and warmth the sympathies of our government, as well as that of your people, makes itself loudly heard as soon as an opportunity presents. . . .

I will add that this sympathy is increased by the re-

⁸ From J. F. Loubat, *Narrative of the Mission to Russia in 1866 of the Hon. Gustavus Vasa Fox. From the Journal and Notes of Loubat*, ed. by John D. Champlin, Jr. (New York: Appleton, 1873), pp. 250-253. 259-260.

semblance of our institutions, by our connections with Europe, and history generally. I do not speak of our likeness as regards the extent of our territory, our power and means; nor of the abundance of our natural productions. As regards institutions, the United States is a republic, and Russia an absolute monarchy; but here, as well as on the map, extremes meet. In the Russian absolute monarchy there is a democratic stream that flows uninterruptedly throughout its history. As regards the forms, all of them have lost much of their original meaning, and our honorable guests have justly remarked in one of their speeches, that under our form one may progress; and they now hear in Moscow what they heard in St. Petersburg, that the Russians, thanks to our gracious emperor—who marks a new era in our history—may express their ideas and reason as freely as people do in New York.

I have but to speak in conclusion, of the resemblance between Russia and the United States in reference to the Old World. It is impossible not to agree that Europe looks on the New World with some apprehension, some suspicion, some jealousy. I believe I make no mistake in asserting that the principal European governments, influenced severally by their own views and particularities— and I do not blame them—did not look at the American conflict [*Civil War*] so impartially and disinterestedly as we did. They rather wished that there should be two Unions instead of one. They regard with the same eyes the other New World—I mean Russia. For fifty years, during the reigns of Alexander I and Nicolai, Russia was the chief supporter of peace in Europe, without regard to her own interests; but as soon as there was an opportunity, all this was forgotten, and Europe, without cause, leagued with Turkey against us, with the only aim of weakening our power by attacking us suddenly, perhaps in the jealousy of her old age, in the general and involuntary conviction that America and Russia will have as much in their future as she has had in her past.

Yes, it is evident, by all the combinations of the science of history, that to Russia, as well as to America, a great future is reserved, to which we are now drawing near, thank God, with hope and faith. Let us wish that the friendly union between the two governments may pass from an ideal to an actual one, so that we may advance hand-in-hand; that both the nations may develop, ripen, and strengthen this idea of mutual cooperation on this glorious road so far as possibility will permit. . . .

Mr. Schipoff, a leading Moscow merchant: . . . With unexampled energy and valor the North American states fought for the abolition of slavery at the same time that Russia was accomplishing the emancipation of twenty million serfs. In the United States self government is developed in the highest degree; and Russia too, is introducing it in her municipal corporations. In the United States courts of justice are open; Russia is establishing the like system, and already the people rejoice at the beneficial effects of its institution. Both countries are great in territory, both contain inexhaustible treasures, but these treasures require development, and this development can only be attained by means of adequately remunerating capital and labor. Of this the United States are fully convinced, and, consequently, in their commercial policy, maintain strictly the principle of protection, not suffering themselves to be misled by the plausible theories of certain economists. Russia, too, is beginning to understand that in strict protection of national labor, in connection with a full development of the resources of a country, lies the secret of national wealth. And by no one has this truth been so clearly and so convincingly put as by that highly-respected American political economist, Carey, and by our own esteemed guest, now for the second time in Moscow, General Clay. Like them, we believe that love toward mankind begins with love toward one's own country, and a proper encouragement of national labor. In whatever direction we turn, we see everywhere that Russia and America are so directed by the hand of Providence that their individual interests not only do not impede, but, on the contrary, promote their mutual development. Consequently, the more Americans and Russians love their country, the nearer they draw toward each other. . . . Here in our ancient capital, replete with true Russian life, let us raise our glasses to the welfare, prosperity, and power of the two nations whom a great future surely awaits.

— Reading No. 9 —

HAXTHAUSEN: *THE MIR AND THE LAND* [9]

Baron August von Haxthausen (1792-1866) a German economist, investigated the rural conditions in Russia in 1843. In his report (published 1847-1852), translated into English in 1856, Haxthausen recognized the mir, *or village commune, as an important Russian institution.*

↗   ↗   ↗

The Russians say that the earth belongs to the Creator, and has been granted by Him to Adam and his descendants. Successive generations inherited the possession; and as their numbers increased they occupied a greater extent of the earth's surface, which they shared under the Divine guidance in the world's history. The country now called Russia fell to the progenitor of the Russians; and his descendants, remaining united under the head of their race, and thus constituting a people, spread over the territory which has thus by the providence of God become their property. The disposal of it, as in a family, belongs to the father, the head of the race, the Czar; an individual has a right to share in it only so long as he lives in unity with the Czar and his people. The soil is the joint property of the national family, and the father or Czar has the sole disposal of it, and distributes it among the families into which the nation in the course of time has been divided. A joint occupancy of the whole could only exist when the people led a nomadic life; when they became settled, a portion was assigned to each family, which occupied its share under a separate head. The right of the family thus arose in a manner quite analogous to that of the

[9] From Baron von Haxthausen, *The Russian Empire, its people, institutions and resources,* tr. by Robert Farie (London: Chapman & Hall, 1856), vol. 2, p. 229 f.

nation. The property is a family property, belonging equally but undivided to all the members of the family, —the father having the disposal and distribution of the produce. If a member insists on a division, he receives his portion, but loses all claim upon the joint possession; he is paid off and excluded, and thenceforth constitutes a new family. The families thus remain for many generations under their respective heads, and became family communes.

The Commune is still considered in law to form a family. If a stranger comes to reside in a village, he is adopted. Every member has an equal claim upon the joint and undivided communal property; the distribution of the produce rests with the fathers, the "White-heads" or *Starosta* (Elders). A member cannot possess private property in the land, therefore cannot bequeath it; but his sons, by virtue of their birth into the family, have an immediate right to a share in the joint property and its usufruct. . . .

The patriarchal government, feelings, and organization are in full activity in the life, manners, and customs of the Great Russians. The same unlimited authority which the father exercises over all his children is possessed by the mother over her daughters: the same reverence and obedience are shown to the Communal authority, the *Starosta* and the White-heads, and to the common father of all, the Czar. The Russian addresses the same word to his real father, to the *Starosta,* to his proprietor, to the Emperor, and finally to God, viz. Father; in like manner he calls every Russian, whether known to him or not, Brother. . . .

The patriarchal ruler or Czar appears necessary to the very existence of the people; we never find an insurrection against the Government of the Czar, against the institution of Czardom, but only against certain persons, and generally upon the grounds of legitimacy, as in the instance of the false Demetrius of Pugatchev, who represented himself as the exiled Peter III, or as in the insurrection of 1825. The people have shown invariable obedience to every government, even to that of the Mongols; they frequently indeed complain of supposed wrongs, but there the matter ends.

The Czar is the father of his people; but the descent,

and even the sex, of the sovereign is indifferent, to them.
The Empress Catherine II, a foreign princess, experienced
the same veneration and attachment as princes born in
Russia; she became nationalized on assuming the Czardom. This profound veneration for authority passes to
the person of every one who assumes the office of
Czar. . . .

— Reading No. 10 —

WALLACE: *SERFS AND EMANCIPATION*[10]

*The observations which Sir Donald Mackenzie Wallace
(1841-1919) made about the conditions and life of the
Russian peasants before and immediately after their
Emancipation (1861) are of great importance.*

✓   ✓   ✓

As to the means which the proprietors possessed of op-
pressing their peasants, we must distinguish between the
legal and the actual. The legal were almost as complete
as any one could desire. "The proprietor," it is said in the
Laws (Vol. IZ., 1045, ed. an. 1857), "may impose on the
serfs every kind of labor, may take from them money
dues (*obrok*) and demand from them personal service,
with this one restriction, that they should not be thereby
ruined, and that the number of days fixed by law should
be left to them for their own work." Besides this, he had
the right to transform peasants into domestic servants,
and might, instead of employing them in his own service,
hire them out to others who had the rights and privileges
of noblesse (1047-48). For all offenses committed against
himself or against any one under his jurisdiction, he
could subject the guilty ones to corporal punishment not

[10] From D. M. Wallace, *Russia* (New York: Holt & Co.,
1877), pp. 478 *ff.*, 500 *ff.*

exceeding forty lashes with the birch or fifteen blows with
the stick (1052); and if he considered any of his serfs as
incorrigible he could present them to the authorities to
be drafted into the army or transported to Siberia as he
might desire (1053-55). In cases of insubordination,
where the ordinary domestic means of discipline did not
suffice, he could call in the police and the military to support his authority.

Such were the legal means by which the proprietor
might oppress his peasants, and it will be readily understood that they were very considerable and very elastic.
By law he had the power to impose any dues in labor or
money which he might think fit, and in all cases the serfs
were ordered to be docile and obedient (1027). Corporal
punishment, though restricted by law, he could in reality
apply to any extent. Certainly none of the serfs, and very
few of the proprietors, were aware that the law placed any
restriction on this right. All the proprietors were in the
habit of using corporal punishment as they thought
proper, and unless a proprietor became notorious for inhuman cruelty, the authorities never thought of interfering. But in the eyes of the peasants corporal punishment
was not the worst. What they feared infinitely more than
the birch or the stick was the proprietor's power of giving them or their sons as recruits. The law assumed that
this extreme means would be employed only against those
serfs who showed themselves incorrigibly vicious or in-
subordinate; but the authorities accepted those presented
without making any investigations, and consequently the
proprietor might use his power as an effective means
of extortion.

Against these means of extortion and oppression the
serfs had no legal protection. The law provided them with
no means of resisting any injustice to which they might
be subjected, or of bringing to punishment the master
who oppressed and ruined them. The Government, notwithstanding its sincere desire to protect them from in-
ordinate burdens and cruel treatment, rarely interfered
between the master and his serfs, being afraid of thereby
undermining the authority of the proprietors, and awakening among the peasantry a spirit of insubordination. The
serfs were left, therefore, to their own resources, and had
to defend themselves as best they could. The simplest way

was open mutiny; but this was rarely employed, for they know by experience that any attempt of the kind would be at once put down by the military and mercilessly punished. Much more favorite and efficient methods were passive resistance, flight, and fire-raising or murder.

We might naturally suppose that an unscrupulous proprietor, armed with the enormous legal and actual power which I have just described, could easily extort from his peasants anything he desired. In reality, however, the process of extortion, when it exceeded a certain measure, was a very difficult operation. The Russian peasant has a capacity of patient endurance that would do honor to a martyr, and a power of continued, dogged, passive resistance such as is possessed, I believe, by no other class of men in Europe; and these qualities formed a very powerful barrier against the rapacity of unconscientious proprietors.

In speaking of the serfs I have hitherto confined my attention to the members of the *Mir,* or rural Commune —that is to say, the peasants in the narrower sense of the terms; but besides these there were the *Dvorovye,* or domestic servants, and of these I must add a word or two.

The Dvorovye were domestic slaves rather than serfs in the proper sense of the word. Let us, however, avoid wounding unnecessarily Russian sensibilities by the use of the ill-sounding word. We may call the class in question "domestics"—remembering, of course, that they were not quite domestic servants in the ordinary sense. They received no wages, were not at liberty to change masters, possessed almost no legal rights, and might be punished, hired out, or sold by their owners without any infraction of the written law.

These "domestics" were very numerous—out of all proportion to the work to be performed—and could consequently lead a very lazy life; but the peasant considered it a great misfortune to be transferred to their ranks, for he thereby lost his share of the Communal land and the little independence which he enjoyed.

It might be reasonably supposed that the serfs received with boundless gratitude and delight the Manifesto proclaiming these principles. Here at last was the realization of their long cherished hopes. Liberty was accorded to them, and not only liberty, but a goodly portion of the soil—more than a half or all the arable land possessed by the proprietors.

In reality the Manifesto created among the peasantry a feeling of disappointment rather than delight. To understand this strange fact we must endeavor to place ourselves at the peasant's point of view.

In the first place, it must be remarked that all vague, rhetorical phrases about free labor, human dignity, national progress, and the like, which may readily produce among educated men a certain amount of temporary enthusiasm, fall on the ears of the Russian peasant like drops of rain on a granite rock. If, therefore, the Government would make a law by which his share of the Communal land would be increased, or his share of the Communal burdens diminished, he would in return willingly consent to be therein designated by the most ugly name that learned ingenuity can devise.

In their minds the proprietors were merely temporary occupants, who were allowed by the Tsar to exact labor and dues from the serfs. What then was Emancipation? Certainly the abolition of all obligatory labor and money dues, and perhaps the complete ejectment of the proprietors. On this latter point there was a difference of opinion. All assumed, as a matter of course, that the Communal land would remain the property of the Commune, but it was not so clear that would be done with the rest of the estate. Some thought that it would be retained by the proprietor, but very many believed that the nobles would receive salaries from the Tsar, and that all the land would be given to the Communes. In this way the Emancipation would be in accordance with historical right and with the material advantage of the peasantry, for whose exclusive benefit, it was assumed, the reform had been undertaken.

Instead of this the peasants found that they were still to pay dues, even for the Communal land which they regarded as unquestionably their own! So at least said the expounders of the law. But the thing was incredible. Either the proprietors must be concealing or misinterpreting the law, or this was merely a preparatory measure, which would be followed by the real Emancipation. Thus were awakened among the peasantry a spirit of mistrust and suspicion and a widespread belief that there would be a

second Emancipation, by which all the land would be
divided and all the dues abolished. . . .

The peasants naturally imagined that, as soon as the
Tsar said they were free, they were no longer obliged to
work for their old masters—that all obligatory labor
ceased as soon as the Manifesto was read. In vain the
proprietors endeavored to convince them that, in regard
to labor, the old relations must continue, as the law en-
joined, until a new arrangement had been made. To all
explanations and exhortations the peasants turned a deaf
ear, and to the efforts of the rural police they too often
opposed a dogged, passive resistance. In many cases the
simple appearance of the authorities sufficed to restore
order, for the presence of one of the Tsar's servants convinced many that the order to work for the present as
formerly was not a mere invention of the proprietors. But
not unfrequently the birch had to be applied. Indeed, I
am inclined to believe, from the numerous descriptions of
this time which I have received from eye-witnessess, that
rarely, if ever, had the serfs seen and experiencd so much
flogging as during these first three months after their liber-
ations. . . .

At first the work of amicable settlement proceeded
slowly. The proprietors generally showed a spirit of concession, and some of them generously proposed conditions much more favorable to the peasants than the law
demanded; but the peasants were filled with vague suspicions, and feared to commit themselves by "putting
pen to paper." Even the highly-respected proprietors, who
imagined that they possessed the unbounded confidence
of the peasantry, were suspected like the others, and their
generous offers were regarded as ill-baited traps. Often I
have heard old men, sometimes with tears in their eyes,
describe the distrust and ingratitude of the peasantry at
this time. Many peasants believed that the proprietors
were hiding the real Emancipation Law, and imaginative
or ill-intentioned persons fostered this belief by professing
to know what the real law contained. The most absurd
rumors were afloat, and whole villages sometimes acted
upon them. In the province of Moscow, for instance, one
Commune sent a deputation to the proprietor to inform
him that, as he had always been a good master, the Mir
would allow him to retain his house and garden during his

lifetime. In another locality it was rumored that the Tsar
sat daily on a golden throne in the Crimea, receiving all
peasants who came to him, and giving them as much land
as they desired; and in order to take advantage of the
Imperial liberality a large body of peasants set out for the
place indicated, and advanced quickly till they were
stopped by the military!

The work of concluding contracts for the redemption
of the dues, or, in other words, for the purchase of the
land ceded in perpetual usufruct, proceeded slowly, and
is, in fact, still going on. The arrangement was as follows:
The dues were capitalized at six per cent., and the Government paid at once to the proprietors four-fifths of the
whole sum. The peasants were to pay to the proprietor
the remaining fifth, either at once or in installments, and
to the Government six percent, for forty-nine years on the
sum advanced. The proprietors willingly adopted this
arrangement, for it provided them with a sum of ready
money, and freed them from the difficult task of collecting
the dues. But the peasants did not show much desire to
undertake the operation. Some of them expected a second
emancipation, and those who did not take this possibility
into their calculations were little disposed to make present sacrifices for distant prospective advantages which
would not be realized for half a century. In most cases
the proprietor was obliged to remit, in whole or in part,
the fifth which was to be paid by the peasants. Many Communes refused to undertake the operation on any conditions, and in consequence of this not few proprietors
demanded the so-called obligatory redemption, according to which they accepted the four-fifth from the Government as full payment, and the operation was thus effected without the peasants being consulted. The total
number of male serfs emancipated was about nine millions and three-quarters, and of these, only about seven
millions and a quarter had already, at the beginning of
1875, made redemption contracts. Of the contracts
signed at that time, about sixty-three percent were "obligatory." . . .

— Reading No. 11 —

WALLACE: *RUSSIAN CITIES IN 1870*[11]

Sir Donald Mackenzie Wallace visited Russia from 1870-1875. He was later foreign correspondent and editor of The Times *(London). His book on Russia is the standard work in English on the little known Russian empire of the 1870's.*

✦ ✦ ✦

At about eighty miles from St. Petersburg the Moscow railway crosses the Volkhof, a rapid, muddy river, which connects Lake Ilmen with Lake Ladoga. At the point of intersection I got on board a small steamer, and sailed up the river for about fifty miles. The journey was tedious, for the country is flat and monotonous, and the steamer did not make more than nine knots an hour. Towards sunset Novgorod appeared on the horizon. Seen thus, in the soft twilight, the town appears decidedly picturesque. On the western bank of the river stands the kremlin, a lightly-elevated piece of ground surrounded by high brick walls, over which peep the painted cupolas of the cathedral. On the opposite bank stands the larger part of the town, the sky-line of which is agreeably broken by the green roofs and pear-shaped cupolas of many churches. Here and there a bit of foliage indicates the existence of gardens. Spanning the river between the kremlin and the town on the opposite bank is a long stone bridge, half hidden by a high temporary wooden bridge, which does duty—or at least did duty at that time—for the older structure. Many people asserted then that the temporary structure was destined to become permanent, because it yielded a comfortable revenue to the officials whose duty it was to keep it in repair; but whether this uncharitable prediction has been realized, I know not.

[11] From D. M. Wallace, *Russia* (New York: Holt & Co., 1877), pp. 165 *ff.*

Those who wish to enjoy the illusions produced by scene-painting and stage-decorations should never go behind the scenes. In like manner he who wishes to preserve the delusion that Russian towns are picturesque should never enter them, but content himself with viewing them from a distance. A walk through the streets inevitably dispels the illusion, and proves satisfactorily that irregularity, even when combined with squalor, is not necessarily picturesque.

However imposing Russian towns may look when seen from the outside, they will generally be found on closer inspection to be little more than villages in disguise. If they have not a positively rustic, they have at least a suburban, appearance. The streets are straight and wide, and are either miserably paved or not paved at all. Trottoirs are not considered indispensable. The houses are built of wood or stone, generally one-storied, and separated from each other by spacious yards. Many of them do not condescend to turn their façades to the street. The general impression produced is that the majority of the burghers have come from the country, and have brought their country houses with them. There are few or no shops with merchandise tastefully arranged in the window to tempt passers-by. If you wish to make purchases you must go to the Gostinny Dvor, or Bazaar, which consists of long symmetrical rows of low-roofed, dimly-lighted stores, with a colonnade in front. This is the place where merchants most do congregate, but it presents nothing of that bustle and activity which we are accustomed to associate with commercial life. The shopkeepers stand at their doors or loiter about in the immediate vicinity waiting for customers. From the scarcity of these latter I should say that when sales are effected the profits must be enormous. In the other parts of the town the air of solitude and languor is still more conspicuous. In the great square, or by the side of the promenade—if the town is fortunate enough to have one —cows or horses may be seen grazing tranquilly, without being at all conscious of the incongruity of their position. And, indeed, it would be strange if they had any such consciousness, for it does not exist in the minds either of the people or of the police or the inhabitants. At night the streets are not lighted at all, or are supplied merely with a few oil-lamps, which do little more than render the darkness visible, so that cautious citizens returning home late often arm themselves with lanterns. A few years ago an honorable town-councilor of Moscow opposed a project for lighting the city with gas, and maintained that those who chose to go out at night, should carry their lamps with them. The objection was overruled, and Moscow was supplied with gas-lamps, but very few of the provincial towns have as yet followed the example of the ancient capital. . . .

The scarcity of towns in Russia is not less remarkable than their rustic appearance. I use the word here in the popular and not in the official sense. In official language a town means a collection of houses, containing certain organs of administration, and hence the term is sometimes applied to petty villages. Let us avoid, then, the official list of the towns, and turn to the statistics of population. It may be presumed, I suppose, that no town is worthy of the name unless it contains at least 10,000 inhabitants. Now, if we apply this test, we shall find that in the whole of European Russia in the narrower sense of the term—excluding Finland, the Baltic provinces, Lithuania, Poland, and the Caucasus, which are politically but not socially parts of Russia—there are only 127 towns. Of these, only twenty-five contain more than 25,-000, and only eleven contain more than 50,000 inhabitants.

These facts indicate plainly that in Russia, as compared with Western Europe, the urban element in the population is relatively small; and this conclusion is borne out by statistical data. In Russia the urban element composes only a tenth part of the entire population, whereas in Great Britain more than one-half of the inhabitants are dwellers in towns. A serious effort to discover the causes of this would certainly bring out some striking peculiarities in the past history and present condition of the Russian Empire.

— Reading No. 12 —

TERROR AND LIBERTY[12]

After the assassination of Emperor Alexander II in March, 1881, the executive committee of the revolutionary organization which had carried through the assassination sent the new emperor Alexander III a lengthy letter in which it promised to abandon all revolutionary activities if Russia would be granted the elementary constitutional liberties. This remarkable letter, sent on March 23, 1881, reads in part:

✦   ✦   ✦

Majesty, although the executive committee understands very well the mood which now possesses you, it does not regard itself justified, out of delicacy, to postpone the following declaration. There are higher duties than even the most justified human feelings: these are the duties toward our country, duties which command every citizen to sacrifice himself, his own sentiments and even those of others. Driven by this imperative duty we address you without hesitation because the development of the events which threaten us for the future with terrible struggles and rivers of blood, does not tolerate any delay.

The tragedy (of Alexander II's assassination) was no accident and should not have surprised anyone. After the events of the last ten years it appears rather as an unavoidable necessity, and the person whom fate has placed at the top of the state should be fully cognizant of its deep significance. Only a man entirely incapable of analysing the life of nations will regard events of this kind as a crime of a few individuals or of a "gang." During a whole decade the revolutionary movement has grown in spite of all the measures taken to suppress it. The best elements of the country, the most energetic

[12] Konni Zilliacus, *Das Revolutionäre Russland* (Frankfurt a. Main: Rütten & Loening, 1905), pp. 128-135.

men of Russia, those most willing to sacrifice themselves,
step forth to enter the ranks of the revolution. For three
years the revolution and the government were linked in
desperate combat.

Your Majesty must agree that the government of the
late tsar could not be accused of a lack of energy. Guilty
and innocent alike were hanged; the jails and the far-off
places of exile were crowded. The so-called leaders of
the revolution were arrested and dozens of them were
executed. They died peacefully and with the tranquillity
of martyrs; but their death did not stop the revolution,
on the contrary, it persistently gained in strength. A revolutionary movement, Your Majesty, does not depend
upon individuals. It is a process carried on by the people, and therefore, gallows, erected for the most energetic
representatives of this process, are equally powerless to
save the obsolete order as the crucifixion of the Savior
could not preserve the decaying ancient world before the
triumph of reforming Christianity. The government may
continue with its arrests and executions as long as it
wishes; it may perhaps succeed in destroying some revolutionary organizations, perhaps even the most important ones. Yet the government will not be able to prevent
the further course of events. It is this course of events
which creates revolutionaries—the general dissatisfaction
among the masses and the development of new social
forms in Russia.

A whole nation cannot be suppressed and the dissatisfaction of a nation can even less be extinguished by mere
severity. On the contrary, severity will increase not only
dissatisfaction but also its energy and its forces. The
latter ones will be better organized with the growth of
experience. Therefore the revolutionary organizations
must in the course of time gain in number and strength.
Finally a terrible explosion, a blood-drenched revolution,
will convulse the whole nation and destroy the old order
of things.

Yes, Your Majesty, this is a sad and terrible perspec-
tive. Please do not think it an empty phrase. We feel
more strongly than anyone else what a misfortune it will
be to lose so many talents and so much energy in destructive and violent conflicts at a time when, under different conditions, the same forces could be employed for

fertile constructive tasks, for the education of the people, for the common weal.

But why then this sad necessity for a sanguinary struggle? For that reason, Majesty, because we have no government in the true sense of the word. For a true government is the expression of the will of the people and we must try to realize the will of the people. In our country, however—kindly excuse the expression—the government has degenerated into a camarilla and it deserves much more the name of a gang of usurpers than we do. Whatever good intentions the emperor may have, the actions of the government have nothing in common with the aspirations and the welfare of the people. The Russian government has brought the masses to such a state of poverty and misery that they haven't even the freedom to act for their common welfare and that even in their own homes they are not safe against secret police.

There are only two ways out of such a situation: a revolution which cannot be prevented by executions, or the voluntary transfer of the supreme power to the people and their participation in the government. In the interests of the country and in order to preclude such a terrible misfortune as a revolution always is, the executive committee appeals to Your Majesty to follow the second alternative. Please be assured that as soon as the supreme power ceases to be an arbitrry power, as soon as it is determined to carry out what the people's will and conscience demand, you can dismiss all your spies who compromise the government, can send your bodyguards back to the barracks, and can burn the gallows which demoralize the people. Then the executive committee will abandon its activity. It will disband its organization and will devote itself to the productive work for civilization and the welfare of the people. The acts of violence which are even more abhorrent to us than to your servants, and to which we are forced only by a sad necessity, will then be replaced by the peaceful competition of ideas.

We turn to you, Your Majesty, forgetting every prejudice and distrust which the government has aroused against itself throughout the centuries. We wish to forget that you represent that power which has deceived the people and done it so much injustice. We turn to you as a fellow citizen and an honest man. We hope that the feeling of personal bitterness will suppress in you neither your feeling of duty nor the will to hear the truth. We too have reasons to feel bitter. You have lost your father, but we have lost not only our fathers but also our brothers, our wives, our sons, and our best friends. Nevertheless we are ready to silence every personal feeling when Russia's welfare demands it and we expect the same from you.

We did not create the conditions which must be fulfilled so that the revolutionary movement gives way to a peaceful development. The events have created them, we only bring them to your attention. These conditions rest upon two fundamental principles: first, a general amnesty for all political criminals, because they have committed no crimes but have simply done their civic duty. Second, the convocation of an assembly of representatives of the whole people to discuss the new foundations of the forms of social and political life, in accordance with the desires and needs of the people.

It is necessary, however, to point out that the elections for such an assembly must be completely free. The representatives shall be chosen from all classes of the population without distinction according to population distribution. There must be no restrictions either on the voters or on their deputies. The agitation for the elections must be entirely free and therefore the government must temporarily grant, until the assembly decides it, complete liberty of press and speech, of assembly, and of electoral programs.

That is the only means of guiding Russia on the road to peaceful and regular development. We solemnly declare before the fatherland and before the whole world, that our party will subordinate itself without any reservations to a national assembly freely elected under the above conditions. We solemnly declare that our party will not allow itself in the future to undertake any violent action against the government sanctioned by the national assembly.

And now, Your Majesty, you must decide for yourself.

Two roads are open before you. The choice is yours.
We can only express the hope that your reason and your
conscience will dictate to you the only decision which is
compatible with Russia's welfare, with your own dignity,
and with your duties toward the fatherland.

— Reading No. 13 —

REVOLUTION, FREEDOM, AND VIOLENCE [13]

    *The following three documents illustrate the attitude
of the Russian revolutionaries in the early 1880's regarding violence and the revolution. The first document is a
letter written by the organization Narodnaya Volya to the
American people in 1880, when it sent an emissary to
the United States to propagate an understanding of the
Russian Revolution. The emissary soon ceased all his activities on the behalf of the Russian Revolution in the
United States and died there more than thirty years later
as a peaceful farmer. The second document was a letter
of condolence by the Narodnaya Volya to the American
people on the occasion of the assassination of President
Garfield. The third document is one of the early manifestations of liberal constitutional thought in Russia with
its rejection of the methods of political terror. Even these
constitutionalists could act and publish only as an illegal
secret organization.*

✓   ✓   ✓

[13] Quoted in Max M. Laserson, *The American Impact on
    Russia—Diplomatic and Ideological—1784-1917* (New
    York: Macmillan, 1950), pp. 197 *f.*, 202, 203.

I

It is difficult for contemporary American society even to conceive what the present situation in Russia actually represents. The unlimited monarchy, the almost contemptuous arbitrariness, and the state order itself which is based on the maxim, "The Emperor is everything, the people nothing," are utterly foreign to the whole spirit of American institutions.

The Russian people in their own country actually equal zero. The entire body of the people is no more than a taxpaying multitude which delivers to despotism the means of its shameful existence, a despotism, moreover, that is supported by forests of bayonets and mountains of bombs. Russian despotism draws its physical power from the people, extracting annually the flower of the youthful workers among the peasantry. Money and soldiers—these are the wellsprings of its very life. If the masses are unable to pay taxes, they are flogged in the markets.

No less sad is the situation of the intellectual class. To sympathize with the people, with their poverty and misfortune, is a heavy crime.

. . . Talented publicists, scholars, littérateurs, and authors whose writings are dedicated to social problems are regarded as enemies of the government and traitors to their country. Many languish in exile, among them, for instance, such a luminary in the world of political economy as Chernyshevsky.

Citizen-democrats! On which side are your sympathies? The reply to this question is for us a foregone conclusion. A country that, at the dawn of its history, has closed its ranks in defense of its independence, a country that has opened its arms to all the persecuted of the European continent, a country that has gone so far as to wage a fratricidal civil war for the sake of the emancipation of millions of slaves, such a country cannot but sympathize with us who have raised the banner of liberation of the Russian people from the chains of political and economic bondage. The abolitionists were your beloved and chosen sons. They really served mankind.

We are the Russian abolitionists! Your sympathies belong undividedly to us! Your indignation and contempt

belong entirely to our enemies! Your sympathies as well
as those of all peoples are cherished by us. We want to
strengthen them.

That is why we intend to make you acquainted with
the actual situation in Russia, with its political as well as
its general aspects. For this purpose we send to your
hospitable country our trusted representative, Leo Hart-
mann. He will report to you the history of our struggle,
its bloody episodes, and the deeds of our martyrs. He
intends to publish brochures and deliver lectures. People
of America! We are confident that he will be received
by you with friendliness and brotherliness.

The Executive Committee

25 Oct. (6 Nov.) 1880

II

Extending to the American people our deep condo-
lences on the occasion of the death of President James
Abram Garfield, the Executive Committee considers it
its duty to express in the name of Russian revolutionaries
its protest against such violent deeds as the attempt of
Guiteau on the life of the President. In a country in
which freedom of the person guarantees full possibility
of an honest struggle of ideas, where a free people's will
not only makes the law but also elects the rulers—in
such a country political murder as an instrument of political conflict is an expression of that very spirit of despotism from which it is our aim to extricate Russia. Personal despotism is as contemptible as party despotism,
and violence can be justified only if it is directed against
violence.

The Executive Committee

September 10, 1881

III

A group of Russian constitutionalists deem it their duty
to address themselves to the multitude who strive for—
or at least sympathize with—the abolition of political
serfdom in our country.

We do not approve the means used by the terrorist
fraction of Russian socialist revolutionaries, and we are
going to fight the government only by means of propa-

ganda and persuasion. Nevertheless, we cannot conscientiously condemn a series of violations and crimes that have been provoked by a centuries-long brutality and mercilessness on the part of the government itself.

The Russian constitutionalists are striving to put an end to the police-state arbitrariness of our government.

— Reading No. 14 —

SOLOVEV: *AGAINST THE SLAVOPHILS* [14]

Vladimir Solovev (1853-1900), Russia's leading philosopher, wrote in 1888 against the Slavophil over-emphasis on Russia's uniqueness and superiority over Europe.

✐   ✐   ✐

Although Russian science and scholarship, whose serious beginnings we can date from Lomonosov [*Mikhail Lomonosov, 1711-1765, the first Russian scientist*], had less time for its development than Western European science, it had on the other hand the great advantage that the Russian scholars found a soil well prepared for them by their European colleagues and could thus build on secure foundations. The Russians have certainly proved their qualifications for every scholarly or scientific activity. These qualifications, together with the excellent training which the Russian scholars received, aroused the hope among the Slavophils, that the Russian nation would accomplish real miracles in the scientific field, in view of the extraordinarliy fast intellectual development of our time. Reality has not fulfilled these

[14] From Hans Kohn, *The Mind of Modern Russia* (New Brunswick, N.J.: Rutgers University Press, 1955), pp. 215, 217, 218, 219 *f*.

hopes. Born under unusually favorable circumstances, Russian scholarship has not been able to make any startlingly new contributions. In mathematics, chemistry, and biology we can, it is true, find some Russian scholars who occupy a considerable and honorable position in the European world of scholarship. Yet their work bears no stamp of a specifically Russian science. It has no sharply defined national character. Moreover, the scientific works of our greatest scholars, in spite of their excellent qualities, are not so profoundly significant as to influence definitively the general course of scientific development. None is of epoch-making importance in the history of even one of the various fields of scientific endeavor. . . .

German idealistic philosophy in its final Hegelian form has nowhere in Europe aroused as much interest and understanding as it has awakened in our educated circles in the thirties and forties. Yet in spite of the enthusiasm that it aroused among so many excellent minds, this philosophic movement bore no fruit. A prominent thinker, Ivan Kireyevsky [1806-1856], came to the conclusion that true wisdom and real science could be found only in the ascetic writers of the Orthodox East. His friends hoped that he would draw from this deep well the living waters of a new Eastern philosophy; and that he would oppose it triumphantly to the desiccated intellectual life of the rotting West. But Kireyevsky failed to produce anything beyond a few general remarks. The entire Russian philosophical movement of that period left nothing but a few essays, which were partly inspired by the outlook of Western philosophers and partly directed against that outlook. These essays, however, contained no positive foundations of an independent and original philosophical system. . . .

Russian intellectual life oscillates between two points of view, an extreme scepticism and an extreme mysticism. It is evident that both points of view preclude a real philosophy. It is true that every profound philosophical system contains a sceptical and a mystical element. Philosophical scepticism is directed against all arbitrary authority and against all apparent reality. Philosophical mysticism is the consciousness of the inner and indestructible connection of the thinking mind with the absolute. But the attitude which underlies Russian thought has no relation to this kind of scepticism or mysticism. Russian scepticism has little in common with the legitimate doubts of Descartes or Kant who wished to find the limits of cognition. Russian scepticism wishes to destroy the idea of truth itself and to undermine the interest in cognition. In a similar way our national mysticism leads to the subordination of our spiritual individuality to an absolute object recognized as something superior. This irretrievable loss of self in a higher entity expresses itself sometimes in an unshakable indifference and passivity and sometimes in a suicidal fanaticism. Under these conditions there can be no foundation for a great and independent Russian future in the field of thought and knowledge.

Without doubt the best examples of Russian creative writing have a specific character and intrinsic value. However, this is also true of German, Spanish, and English literature; and yet these qualities do not imply a special cultural-historical type of these nations. Why should it do so for Russia? Nobody contests the existence of a Russian national character which manifests itself, among other things, in literature. The Russian and the English novel certainly differ, but not more than the English and Spanish. The Russian novel represents one type among the many types of European novels. And as Russian literature can be regarded only as a form of European literature, so Russia, in spite of her distinctive character, is only a European state among the other European states. Danilevsky's contrary position cannot adduce a single proof for its point of view.

In periods of national egoism and isolation from the rest of the Christian world, Russia has not been able to produce anything great or significant. Only through the closest internal and external ties with Europe can Russia become great. . . .

Danilevsky opens his book "Russia and Europe" with the question, "Why doesn't Europe love Russia?" His answer is well known. Europe, he thinks, fears us as a new and higher cultural-historical type which is destined to replace the obsolescent Roman-Germanic civilization. However, the contents of his book and his own confessions suggest another answer. Europe views Russia with hostility and anxiety, for she recognizes the dark and

enigmatic elemental forces alive in the Russian people,
and, together with Russia's spiritual and cultural poverty,
that country's vast and well defined ambition. Europe
fears above all the voice of our "nationalism," a nationalism which desires to destroy Turkey and Austria, to di-
vide Germany, to annex Constantinople, and, should an
opportunity arise, even India. If, however, we are asked
what we have to offer mankind as compensation for what
we take and destroy, what spiritual and cultural principles we have contributed to world history, then we must
either be silent or indulge in meaningless phrases.

If Danilevsky's bitter confession that Russia is a "sick
and enfeebled colossus," is true, then the question "Why
doesn't Europe love us?" must be replaced by a more
obvious and important one, namely, "What is the nature
and cause of our malady?" Physically Russia is strong
enough, as the last Russian war in the East [1877-78]
has demonstrated. Our illness must therefore be of a
moral nature. We carry the burden, as an old writer
says, of our people's sins, which we do not wish to acknowledge. That is a fact which must be foremost in
our minds. As long as we remain morally crippled, our
elemental energies can only harm us. Therefore the most
important, nay, the only important question for a true,
clear-sighted Russian patriot, is not the question of our
power or of our mission, but the question of "Russia's
sin." . . .

— Reading No. 15 —

POBYEDONOSTSEV: *FALLACY OF WESTERN DEMOCRACY* [15]

[15] From K. P. Pobyedonostsev, *Reflections of a Russian
Statesman,* tr. by R. C. Long, preface by Olga Novikoff
(London: Grant Richards, 1898).

In 1896 Pobyedonostsev published Moskovsky Sbornik *which was translated two years later into English. It is a sharp criticism of Western civilization and its institutions in contrast to the Russian national ideal. According to him, parliamentary democracy necessarily led to moral degradation, and freedom of speech and press meant the right to lie and to pervert the people's minds.*

✓   ✓   ✓

In a Democracy, the real rulers are the dexterous manipulators of votes, with their placemen, the mechanics who so skillfully operate the hidden strings which move the puppets in the arena of democratic elections. Men of this kind are ever ready with loud speeches lauding equality; in reality, they rule the people as any despot or military dictator might rule it. The extension of the right to participate in elections is regarded as progress and as the conquest of freedom by democratic theorists, who hold that the more numerous the participants in political rights, the greater is the probability that all will employ this right in the interests of the public welfare, and for the increase of the freedom of the people. Experience proves a very different thing. The history of mankind bears witness that the most necessary and fruitful reforms— the most durable measures—emanated from the supreme will of statesmen, or from a minority enlightened by lofty ideas and deep knowledge, and that, on the contrary, the extension of the representative principle is accompanied by an abasement of political ideas and the vulgarisation of opinions in the mass of the electors. It shows also that this extension—in great States—was inspired by secret aims to the centralization of power, or led directly to dictatorship. In France, universal suffrage was suppressed with the end of the Terror, and was re-established twice merely to affirm the autocracy of the two Napoleons. In Germany, the establishment of universal suffrage served merely to strengthen the high authority of a famous statesman who had acquired popularity by the success of his policy. What its ultimate consequences will be, Heaven only knows! . . .

In what does the theory of Parliamentarism consist? It is supposed that the people in its assemblies makes its own laws, and elects responsible officers to execute its will. Such is the ideal conception. Its immediate realisation is impossible. The historical development of society necessitates that local communities increase in numbers and complexity; that separate races be assimilated, or, retaining their polities and languages, unite under a single flag, that territory extend indefinitely: under such conditions direct government by the people is impracticable. The people must, therefore, delegate its right of power to its representatives, and invest them with administrative autonomy. These representatives in turn cannot govern immediately, but are compelled to elect a still smaller number of trustworthy persons—ministers—to whom they entrust the preparation and execution of the laws, the apportionment and collection of taxes, the appointment of subordinate officials, and the disposition of the militant forces.

In the abstract this mechanism is quite symmetrical: for its proper operation many conditions are essential. . . . Given such conditions the machine would work exactly, and would accomplish its purpose. The law would actually embody the will of the people: administrative measures would actually emanate from Parliament; the pillars of the State would rest actually on the elective assemblies, and each citizen would directly and consciously participate in the management of public affairs.

Such is the theory. Let us look at the practice. Even in the classic countries of Parliamentarism it would satisfy not one of the conditions enumerated. The elections in no way express the will of the electors. The popular representatives are in no way restricted by the opinions of their constituents, but are guided by their own views and considerations, modified by the tactics of their opponents. In reality, ministers are autocratic, and they rule, rather than are ruled by, Parliament. They attain power, and lose power, not by virtue of the will of the people, but through immense personal influence, or the influence of a strong party which places them in power, or drives them from it. They dispose of the force and resources of the nation at will, they grant immunities and favours, they maintain a multitude of idlers at the expense

of the people, and they fear no censure while they enjoy
the support in Parliament of a majority which they maintain by the distribution of bounties from the rich tables
which the State has put at their disposal. In reality, the
ministers are as irresponsible as the representatives of the
people. Mistakes, abuse of power, and arbitrary acts, are
of daily occurrence, yet how often do we hear of the
grave responsibility of a minister? It may be once in
fifty years a minister is tried for his crimes, with a result
contemptible when compared with the celebrity gained
by the solemn procedure. . . .

Thus the representative principle works in practice.
The ambitious man comes before his fellow-citizens, and
strives by every means to convince them that he more
than any other is worthy of their confidence. What motives impel him to this quest? It is hard to believe that
he is impelled by disinterested zeal for the public
good. . . .

On the day of polling few give their votes intelligently;
these are the individuals, influential electors whom it has
been worth while to convince in private. The mass of
electors, after the practice of the herd, votes for one of
the candidates nominated by the committees. Not one
exactly knows the man, or considers his character, his
capacity, his convictions; all vote merely because they
have heard his name so often. It would be vain to struggle against this herd. If a level-headed elector wished to
act intelligently in such a grave affair, and not to give
way to the violence of the committee, he would have to
abstain altogether, or to give his vote for his candidate
according to his conviction. However he might act, he
could not prevent the election of the candidate favoured
by the mass of frivolous, indifferent, and prejudiced
electors.

In theory, the elected candidate must be the favourite
of the majority; in fact, he is the favourite of a minority,
sometimes very small, but representing an organised
force, while the majority, like sand, has no coherence,
and is therefore incapable of resisting the clique and the
faction. In theory, the election favours the intelligent and
capable; in reality, it favours the pushing and impudent.
It might be thought that education, experience, conscien-
tiousness in work, and wisdom in affairs, would be es-

sential requirements in the candidate; in reality, whether these qualities exist or not, they are in no way needed in the struggle of the election, where the essential qualities are audacity, a combination of impudence and oratory, and even some vulgarity, which invariably acts on the masses; modesty, in union with delicacy of feeling and thought, is worth nothing. . . .

. . . What is a Parliamentary party? In theory, it is an alliance of men with common convictions, joining forces for the realisation of their views in legislation and administration. But this description applies only to small parties; the large party, which alone is an effective force in Parliament, is formed under the influence only of personal ambition, and centres itself around one commanding personality. By nature, men are divided into two classes—those who tolerate no power above them, and therefore of necessity strive to rule others; and those who by their nature dread the responsibility inseparable from independent action, and who shrink from any resolute exercise of will. These were born for submission, and together constitute a herd, which follows the men of will and resolution, who form the minority. Thus the most talented persons submit willingly, and gladly entrust to stronger hands the control of affairs and the moral responsibility for their direction. Instinctively they seek a leader, and become his obedient instruments, inspired by the conviction that he will lead them to victory—and, often, to spoil. Thus all the important actions of Parliament are controlled by the leaders of the party, who inspire all decision, who lead in combat, and profit by victory. The public sessions are no more than a spectacle for the mass. Speeches are delivered to sustain the fiction of Parliamentarism, but seldom a speech by itself affects the decision of Parliament in a grave affair. Speechmaking serves for the glory of orators, for the increase of their popularity, and the making of their careers; only on rare occasions does it affect the distribution of votes. Majorities and minorities are usually decided before the session begins. Such is the complicated mechanism of the Parliamentary farce; such is the great political lie which dominates our age. . . .

Such is the Parliamentary institution, exalted as the

summit and crown of the edifice of State. It is sad to
think that even in Russia there are men who aspire to
the establishment of this falsehood among us; that our
professors glorify to their young pupils representative
government as the ideal of political science; that our
newspapers pursue it in their articles and feuilletons,
under the name of justice and order, without troubling
to examine without prejudice the working of the parliamentary machine. Yet even where centuries have sanc-
tified its existence, faith already decays; the Liberal intelligence exalts it, but the people groans under its
despotism, and recognizes its falsehood. We may not see,
but our children and grandchildren assuredly will see, the
overthrow of this idol, which contemporary thought in
its vanity continues still to worship. . . .

— Reading No. 16 —

KENNAN: *EXILE IN SIBERIA*[16]

*George Kennan (1845-1924) visited Siberia in 1885
as correspondent of the* Century *Magazine. His report
drew the attention of Europe to the system of Russian
penal administration which existed under the Tsars and
has been greatly expanded under Stalin.*

✓   ✓   ✓

In the year 1880 the well-known and gifted Russian
novelist Vladimir Korolenko, two of whose books have

[16] From G. Kennan, *Siberia and the Exile System* (New
York: The Century Co., 1891), vol. 1, pp. 242 *ff.*

recently been translated into English, was exiled to Eastern Siberia as a result of what the Government itself finally admitted to be an official mistake. Through the influence of Prince Imeretinski, Mr. Korolenko succeeded in getting this mistake corrected before he reached his ultimate destination and was released in the West Siberian city of Tomsk. Hardly had he returned, however, to European Russia, when he was called upon to take the oath of allegiance to Alexander III, and to swear that he would betray every one of his friends or acquaintances whom he knew to be engaged in revolutionary or anti-Government work. No honorable and self-respecting man could take such an oath as that, and of course Mr. Korolenko declined to do so. He was thereupon exiled by administrative process to the East Siberian territory of Yakutsk, where, in a wretched native uius, he lived for about three years. . . .

The grotesque injustice, the heedless cruelty, and the preposterous "mistakes" and "misunderstandings" that make the history of administrative exile in Russia seem to an American like the recital of a wild nightmare, are due to the complete absence, in the Russian form of Government, of checks upon the executive power, and the almost equally complete absence of official responsibility for unjust or illegal action. The Minister of the Interior, in dealing with politicals, is almost wholly unrestrained by law; and as it is utterly impossible for him personally to examine all of the immense number of political cases that come to him for final decision, he is virtually forced to delegate a part of his irresponsible power to chiefs of police, chiefs of gendarmes, governors of provinces, and subordinates in his own administration. They in turn are compelled, for similar reasons, to intrust a part of their authority and discretion to officers of still lower grade; and the latter, who often are stupid, ignorant, or unscrupulous men, are the persons who really make the investigations, the searches, and the examinations upon which the life or liberty of an accused citizen may depend. Theoretically the Minister of the Interior, aided by a council composed of three of his own subordinates and two officers from the Ministry of Justice, reviews and re-examines the cases of all political offenders who are dealt with by administrative process; but practically he does nothing of the kind, and it is impossible that he should do anything of the kind for the very simple reason that he has not the time. . . .

— Reading No. 17 —

TOLSTOY: *OPEN LETTER TO NICOLAI II* [17]

In 1902 Tolstoy sent an open letter to the emperor protesting governmental repression and the lawlessness of life in Russia. Part of the letter reads:

✓   ✓   ✓

A third of the whole of Russia lives under emergency legislation, and that means without any lawful guarantees. The armies of the regular police and of the secret police are continuously growing in numbers. The prisons and penal colonies are overcrowded with thousands of convicts and political criminals, among whom the industrial workers are now included. The censorship issues the most meaningless interdictions, as it had not even been done in the worst times of the 1840's [*under Nicolai I*]. At no previous time have the religious persecutions been so frequent and so cruel as they are today, and they still grow more frequent and more cruel. In all cities and industrial centers soldiers are employed and equipped with live ammunition to be sent out against the people. In many places fratricidal blood has already been shed; everywhere, new and even more cruel events are irresistibly in preparation. Yet this strenuous and terrible

[17] Quoted by one of the Russian contributors in Josef Melnik, ed., *Russen über Russland. Ein Sammelwerk* (Frankfurt am Main: Rütten & Loening, 1906), pp. 442 f.

activity of the government results only in the growing
impoverishment of the rural population, of those 100
million souls on whom the power of Russia is founded,
and who, in spite of the ever increasing budgets, or perhaps on account of the increases, are faced with famine
which has become a normal condition. A similar normal
condition is the general dissatisfaction of all classes with
the government and their open hostility against it.

— Reading No. 18 —

MELNIK: *THE HOPE OF 1905* [18]

*In October, 1905, while the Revolution was still in
progress in Russia, Josef Melnik published an important
volume of essays on Russia written by Russians, in which
all aspects of Russian life and society were analyzed. He
prefaced the volume with the following words, expressing
the great hope which the friends of Russia felt at the
time of the Revolution of 1905.*

♪   ♪   ♪

It is superfluous to stress the importance of the present
work which offers to the European the necessary pre-
requisites to an understanding of the historical events
which take place at present in Russia. Alexander Herzen,
whose name must never remain unmentioned when one
talks of Russian liberty and Russian misery, once said
that Caesar knew the Gauls better than Europe knows
the Russians.

In view of the wide-spread interest in the historical
development of the Russian empire, I thought it advisa-

[18] Josef Melnik, editor, *Russen über Russland. Ein Sammelwerk* (Frankfurt am Main: Rütten & Loening, 1906), pp.
ix f.

ble to produce a symposium in which several prominent
Russians would discuss the situation and the tasks which
confront their fatherland. The fields in which they work
and the opinions which they have of the present and the
future state of Russia are very different. Yet in one point
they all agree. They all join in the same cry: down with
absolutism!

For more than a century this cry has resounded in
Russian history with varying degrees of intensity. Since
the uprising of the Decembrists it has never been completely muted. But due to national and historical peculiarities, Russian life advances only slowly. It is given to
our time to witness the downfall of the dishonored Asian
despotism of St. Petersburg.

Freedom has not yet been conquered, the power of
the unlimited arbitrariness of the autocracy has not yet
been entirely broken, but in the midst of the decisive
struggle, in the midst of innumerable human sacrifices,
the fumes of whose blood rise toward the melancholy
Russian sky, we hear the subterranean bells of the revolution toll old Russia to its grave.

Russia needs liberty not as an arena for the struggle
of political parties for power and influence but to allow
her to tread new paths in the religious and cultural fields,
in her intellectual and economic life.

I dedicate this work to the memory of Anton Chekhov
because he has mourned, like few others, the wretched-
ness and servility of Russian life. He has given poignant
and unforgettable expression to this mourning in his
poetical creations. His profound humanity and the re-
deeming sympathy of his great all-comprehending heart
shone like a light in the dark days of general resignation.
His tender melodies penetrated our souls with an uneasy
longing out of which rose the desire for new forms of
life. He has taught us to hope and to love in a country
where there is so much hopelessness and hatred which
dominate life. His works heralded the mighty thaw and
the rising spring floods which filled us with the anticipation of that which now seeks to burst forth to become
reality.

With reverence and love, we bow before the memory
of the poet. Turning toward the living, we call from the
depths of our soul: May "The land of the slaves, the

land of the masters" (Lermontov) become the land of
free men!

— Reading No. 19 —

KOKOVTSOV: GOVERNMENT AND
DUMA[19]

*The hostile attitude of the government to any reform
was shown in the appointment of Ivan Logginovich
Goremykin (1839-1918) as Prime Minister in 1906 and
again in the critical war years 1914-16. Vladimir Niko-
latwich Kokovtsov who was Minister of Finance 1904-
1914 and Prime Minister 1911-14, himself a Conservative, describes the gulf separating the government from
the parliament.*

      ✓   ✓   ✓

Several times during our conversation of nearly an
hour, the Tsar expressed his hope that the Duma, faced
with the responsibility of legislative work, would prove
itself less revolutionary than I feared. He was especially
hopeful that the zemstvo people, who seemed to have
acquired a dominant position in the Duma, would not
want to take the lead in a new struggle between the government and the representatives of the people. I pointed
out that I had been out of Russia for some time, did not
have adequate information, and therefore might be mistaken: nevertheless, I believed that if this were true the
needs of the moment hardly called for a new chairman
of the Ministers' Council. The Tsar asked me to explain
myself more clearly, saying why I thought Goremykin

[19] From *Out of My Past. The Memoirs of Count Kokovtsov,*
    ed. by H. H. Fisher (Stanford: Stanford University Press,
    1935), pp. 126-131. Reprinted by permission.

so poorly fitted to cope with the present situation and to feel no restraint because his decision had already been made. Our conversation on this subject became prolonged. I frankly expressed to the Tsar all my fears that Ivan Logginovich's personality, his great indifference toward everything, his utter inability to compromise, and his outspoken unwillingness to meet new elements of our state life would not only fail to help us get acquainted with them but would serve to increase the opposition. The Tsar listened to me calmly, raised a few objections, and finally said that I might be right but that it could no longer be helped since he had offered Goremykin the office and could not withdraw his offer. He was sure, however, that Goremykin would retire whenever he saw that his retirement would help to mend the relations with the new Duma. "What is most important to me," said the Emperor, "is that Goremykin will not act behind my back, making concessions and agreements to damage my authority. I can be perfectly confident that I shall not be given any surprises or made to face any faits accomplis, as was the case with the electoral laws. And that was not the only case." . . .

Late in the evening of April 25, as we were sitting at home among a few close friends, the doorbell rang and I was handed a package. It contained the ukase appointing me Minister of Finance and a program of ceremonies of the opening of the Duma and the State Council by the Emperor in the Winter Palace. . . .

St. George's Room, the throne room, presented a queer spectacle at this moment, and I believe its walls had never before witnessed such a scene. The entire right side of the room was filled with uniformed people, members of the State Council, and the Tsar's retinue. The left side was crowded with the members of the Duma, a small number of whom had appeared in full dress, while the overwhelming majority, occupying the first places near the throne, were dressed as if intentionally in workers' blouses and cotton shirts, and behind them was a crowd of peasants in the most varied costumes, some in national dress, and a multitude of representatives of the clergy. The first place among these representatives of the people was occupied by a man of tall stature, dressed in a workers' blouse and high, oiled boots, who

examined the throne and those about it with a derisive
and insolent eye. It was the famous F. M. Onipko, who
later won great renown by his bold statements in the
first Duma and who also played a prominent role in the
Kronstadt insurrection. While the Tsar read his speech
addressed to the newly elected members of the Duma, I
could not take my eyes off Onipko, so much contempt
and hate did his insolent face show. . . .

The Dowager Empress accorded me a totally different
reception. She began by saying that she had seen me
during the "terrible reception," that she was still unable
to calm herself after having seen all these new people
filling the rooms of the palace for the first time. "They
looked at us," she said, "as upon their enemies, and I
could not make myself stop looking at certain faces, so
much did they seem to reflect an incomprehensible hatred
for all of us." Then she asked me my opinion as to the
possibility of the government's working with a Duma of
such a composition. To this I replied briefly, stating my
own apprehensions and the general belief that a situation
would soon arise in which we should have to decide either
to introduce a full-fledged parliamentary system, trans-
ferring the power from the Emperor's tried servants to
the representatives of public opinion, or to dissolve the
Duma and prepare a new electoral law.

"All this frightens me greatly," she rejoined, "and I
ask myself if we would be able to protect ourselves from
new revolutionary outbursts, if we have enough strength
to suppress another revolt as we did in Moscow, and if
Goremykin is indeed the man to be of use at such a
moment?"

I answered that I did not think Goremykin himself
believed that he was called upon to play such a part, nor
could I understand why he did not decline his appointment.

This ended our conversation. In parting the Empress
said, "Now I understand why you have so insistently
asked the Tsar not to appoint you; but I also see that
my poor son has very few people whom he can trust,
while you have always told him the truth."

That same day the Duma held an opening session in
its new quarters, and all ministers were invited to attend
a solemn Te Deum at the Taurida Palace at three o'clock.

It was supposed that this would be the first meeting of the people's representatives with the government.

This expectation was realized, but inauspiciously. After the Te Deum we stood in a distinctly secluded group, and no one approached us except Count Heyden, who had known me during his work in the Office of Applications. He alone gave us a few words of greeting, but did not stop to talk, and after a few minutes all of us departed, each one to go his separate way.

— Reading No. 20 —

LENIN: *THE REVOLUTION OF 1905* [20]

In a lecture which he delivered before young socialists in Zurich, Switzerland, in January, 1917, on the twelfth anniversary of the "Bloody Sunday," Lenin said:

A few brief remarks concerning the world significance of the Russian Revolution (of 1905).

Geographically, economically, and historically, Russia belongs, not only to Europe, but also to Asia. This is why the Russian Revolution succeeded in finally rousing the biggest and the most backward country in Europe, and in creating a revolutionary people led by a revolutionary proletariat. It achieved more than that.

The Russian Revolution gave rise to a movement throughout the whole of Asia. The revolutions in Turkey, Persia and China prove that the mighty uprising of 1905 left deep traces, and that its influence expressed in the forward movement of hundreds and hundreds of millions of people is ineradicable.

[20] From *A Handbook of Marxism* (New York: International Publishers, 1935), pp. 632-634.

In an indirect way the Russian Revolution exercised influence also on the countries situated to the west. One must not forget that news of the Tsar's constitutional manifesto, reaching Vienna on October 30, 1905, played a decisive role in the final victory of universal suffrage in Austria.

Very often we meet Western Europeans who argue about the Russian Revolution as if events, relationships, and methods of struggle in that backward country have very little resemblance to Western European relationships and, therefore, can hardly have any practical significance.

There is nothing more erroneous than such an opinion.

No doubt the forms and occasions for the impending battles in the coming European revolution will, in many respects, differ from the forms of the Russian Revolution.

Nevertheless, the Russian Revolution—precisely because of its proletarian character in that particular sense to which I referred—was the prologue to the coming European revolution. Undoubtedly this coming revolution can only be a proletarian revolution in the profounder sense of the word: a proletarian Socialist revolution even in its content. This coming revolution will show to an even greater degree on the one hand, that only stern battles, only civil wars, can free humanity from the yoke of capital; on the other hand, that only class-conscious proletarians can and will come forth in the role of leaders of the vast majority of the exploited.

The present grave-like stillness (1917) in Europe must not deceive us. Europe is charged with revolution. The monstrous horrors of the imperialist war, the suffering caused by the high cost of living, engender everywhere a revolutionary spirit; and the ruling classes, the bourgeoisie with its servitors, the governments, are more and more moving into a blind alley from which they can never extricate themselves without tremendous upheavals.

Just as in 1905 a popular uprising against the Tsarist government commenced under the leadership of the proletariat with the aim of achieving a democratic republic, so the coming years, precisely because of this predatory war, will lead in Europe to popular uprisings under the leadership of the proletariat against the power of finance capital, against the big banks, against the capitalists; and these upheavals cannot end otherwise than with the expropriation of the bourgeoisie, with the victory of Socialism.

We of the older generation may not live to see the decisive battles of this coming revolution. But I can certainly express the hope that the youth who are working so splendidly in the Socialist movement of Switzerland, and of the whole world, will be fortunate enough not only to fight, but also to win, in the coming proletarian revolution.

— Reading No. 21 —

NICOLAI II: DECLARATION OF ABDICATION[21]

As a delegate to the duma, Guchkov went to the headquarters at Pskov where the emperor, on March 15, 1917, signed the document of his abdication. The abdication was dated according to the Julian calendar, March 2, at 15:05 o'clock, countersigned by the Minister of the Imperial Court and addressed to the Chief of the General Staff.

    ✓   ✓   ✓

In the days of the great struggle against the foreign enemies, who for nearly three years have tried to enslave our fatherland, the Lord God has been pleased to send down on Russia a new heavy trial. Internal popular disturbances threaten to have a disastrous effect on the future conduct of this persistent war. The destiny of Russia, the honor of our heroic army, the welfare of the people and the whole future of our dear fatherland de-

[21] Translated from the Russian original reproduced in Paul Herre, *Weltgeschichte der neuesten Zeit* (Leipzig, 1927), vol. II, p. 776.

mand that the war should be brought to a victorious conclusion whatever the cost. The cruel enemy is making his
last efforts, and already the hour approaches when our
glorious army together with our gallant allies will crush
him. In these decisive days in the life of Russia, We
thought it Our duty of conscience to facilitate for Our
people the closest union possible and a consolidation of
all national forces for the speedy attainment of victory.
In agreement with the Imperial Duma We have thought
it well to renounce the Throne of the Russian Empire
and to lay down the supreme power. As We do not wish
to part from Our beloved son, We transmit the succession to Our brother, the Grand Duke Michael Alexandrovich, and give Him Our blessing to mount the
Throne of the Russian Empire. We direct Our brother
to conduct the affairs of state in full and inviolable union
with the representatives of the people in the legislative
bodies on those principles which will be established by
them, and on which He will take an inviolable oath.

In the name of Our dearly beloved homeland, We call
on Our faithful sons of the fatherland to fulfill their sacred duty to the fatherland, to obey the tsar in the heavy
moment of national trials, and to help Him, together
with the representatives of the people, to guide the Russian Empire on the road to victory, welfare, and glory.
May the Lord God help Russia!

— Reading No. 22 —

KAUTSKY: *LENIN AND THE 1917 REVOLUTION*[22]

[22] From Karl Kautsky, *Social Democracy versus Communism*,
ed. by David Shub and Joseph Shaplen, with an introduction by Sidney Hook (New York: The Rand School
Press, 1946), pp. 52-54, 57-61, 64-66.

Karl Kautsky (1854-1938) was one of the leaders of the German Social Democratic Party and its foremost orthodox Marxist theoretician. At one time Lenin hailed him as the only one among Western socialists who understood Russia and its problems. From his knowledge of Marxism and Russia, Kautsky discussed the events of 1917 and Lenin's rise to power.

✓   ✓   ✓

The Social Democracy of Russia was conceived as a democratic organization, in accordance with Marxian principles. But Lenin soon discovered that this was a mistake. He began to demand ever greater powers for the central organ of the party and increasingly circumscribed powers for the membership.

Paul Axelrod, . . . Julius Martov and, later, George Plekhanov opposed him. Even Rosa Luxemburg, who was more inclined to side with him in other matters, expressed misgivings on the score of dictatorship which Lenin sought to introduce in the party.

In his pamphlet "One Step Forward, Two Steps Backward" (1904) Lenin went so far as to assert:

"Bureaucratism against democracy—that must be the organizational principle of the revolutionary Social-Democracy against the organizational principle of the opportunists." (P. 51)

I take the following from a criticism of Lenin by Rosa Luxemburg in "Die Neue Zeit" (XXII.2). She declared:

"The establishment of centralization in the Social Democracy on the basis of blind obedience, to the very smallest detail, to a central authority, in all matters of party organization and activity; a central authority which does all the thinking, attends to everything and decides everything; a central authority isolating the centre of the party from the surrounding revolutionary milieu—as demanded by Lenin— . . . are calculated principally to promote control of party activity and not its development, to foster the limitation rather than the growth, the strangulation rather than the solidarity and expansion of the movement." (Pp. 488, 492)

That was how Rosa Luxemburg characterized Leninism from its very beginning. . . . For this reason, as early as 1904, Rosa Luxemburg perceived Leninism as an element inimical to the higher development of the working class. Naturally, she could not then foresee all the destructive influences it carried within itself.

In the meantime, at the very beginning of Leninism, another extremely injurious element became apparent side by side with its strangulations and stifling of the movement.

Like the God of monotheists, the dictator is a very jealous god. He tolerates no other gods but himself. Those in the party who do not believe in his divine infallibility provoke his fierce hatred. Lenin demanded that the entire working class submit meekly to his leadership. Those in the party who were inclined to show more confidence in other leaders or to defend opinions of their own were regarded by Lenin as the worst possible enemies, to be fought with any and all means. . . .

Whenever dictatorship assumes powers in a party organism, that organism is bound to deteriorate intellectually, for dictatorship either degrades the best elements, compelling them to surrender their independence, or expels them from the party. . . .

Lenin's aim in the Russian Revolution was to destroy not only all organs of self-administration, but also all other parties and social organizations, except his own.

To this end he employed falsehood, slender and brutal force against all opponents, among whom he counted all Socialists, except those who were willing to obey his commands. He finally succeeded in smashing all his opponents through his coup d'état of November 7, 1917. He hoped that the elections to the All Russian Constituent Assembly, which were then in progress, would bring him a majority.

Until 1917 the Bolshevist Party regarded the dictatorship within its organization as a means of struggle for democracy in the state, and Lenin's fight for democracy in the state proceeded along the line of the other socialist parties. Like the latter, as late as 1917, he demanded the convocation of a Constituent Assembly on the basis of universal suffrage.

The elections to the Constituent Assembly revealed

that the Bolshevist Party had far from a majority in the Constituent Assembly. But the Socialist parties—Mensheviks, Bolsheviks and Social Revolutionists—constituted an overwhelming majority in the assembly. Once more the Bolsheviks had an opportunity to take part in a Socialist united front, which could be the basis of a government supported by the overwhelming majority of the people. A government founded on such a basis and having virtually the entire people behind it would have been in a position to crush without any difficulty any attempt at counter-revolution. In fact, any such attempt would have been nipped in the bud.

Had the Bolsheviks at that time agreed to a united front, Russia would have been spared the three years of civil war and the consequent horrible misery. Peace and freedom would have made possible rapid economic recovery and with it a speedy development of the working class, which, in turn, would have promoted the realization of a large measure of Socialist economy and its successful administration. All this would have been possible without dictatorship, without terror, through the democracy of the workers and peasants. To be sure, we cannot say with certainty that this would have actually come to pass, but this was the only road that offered a possibility of obtaining for the people through the revolution as great a measure of liberty and welfare as existing circumstances permitted. But this would have been possible only through the establishment of a revolutionary government supported by the overwhelming majority of the population. Such a government could have been set up only on the basis of a united front of all Socialist parties.

This united front was rendered impossible by the insatiable yearning for power on the part of Lenin and other leaders of the Bolsheviks. They dissolved the Constituent Assembly, which they themselves had previously so passionately championed, and with the help of the politically inexperienced and ignorant soldiery drawn from the disorganized army, whose support they had won by limitless and irresponsible promises, they succeeded in seizing power, by means of which they strengthened their own party, organized on militarist lines, and crushed completely all their opponents. . . .

Upon the ruins of democracy, for which Lenin had

fought until 1917, he erected his political power. Upon
these ruins he set up a new militarist-bureaucratic police
machinery of state, a new autocracy. This gave him weapons against the other Socialists even more potent than
shameless lies. He now had in his hands all the instruments
of repression which czarism had used, adding to these
weapons also those instruments of oppression which the
capitalist, as the owner of the means of production, uses
against wage slaves. Lenin now commanded all the means
of production, utilizing his state power for the erection
of his state capitalism.

No form of capitalism makes the workers so absolutely
dependent upon it as centralized state capitalism in a
state without an effective democracy. And no political
police is so powerful and omnipresent as the Cheka or
G.P.U., created by men who had spent many years in
fighting the czarist police, and knowing its methods as well
as its weaknesses and shortcomings, knew also how to
improve upon them.

It would have been absolutely unnecessary to resort to
any of these instruments of repression had Lenin agreed
to form a coalition with the Mensheviks and Social Revolutionists in 1917. Everything of a truly progressive nature
which the Bolsheviks sought at that time to realize was
also part of the program of the other Socialist parties and
would have been carried out by them, for the people had
empowered them to do so. The confiscation of the big
landed estates had also been planned by the Social
Revolutionists and Mensheviks—they actually put it into
effect in Georgia. Abolition of illiteracy, marriage law
reform, social welfare measures, children's homes, public
hospitals, shop councils, unemployment insurance and
laws for the protection of labor, about all of which such
a big-to-do is being made in Soviet Russia, have been
attained to a much greater and more perfect degree in
capitalist countries where the democracy of labor has won
any considerable power. The socialization of heavy industry, insofar as this would have appeared economically
advantageous, would likewise have been approved by
the majority of the Constituent Assembly.

In the election to the Constituent Assembly 36,000,000
votes were cast, of which only 4,000,000 were polled by
the bourgeois parties and 32,000,000 by the socialist

parties. The Assembly was in no way threatened from the right. It was in a position to proceed undisturbed, with full hope of success, with the task of the regeneration of Russia and preparation for Socialism.

As the Bolsheviks saw it, it had but one great fault: they had failed to obtain a majority in it. The Bolsheviks received 9,000,000, while 23,000,000 votes were cast for the other Socialist parties. This was an intolerable situation for any brave Bolshevik. The Constituent Assembly would have carried out everything in the interests of labor that was at all realizable, and in more rational, more successful manner than the Bolsheviks acting alone have been able to do. But this would have required the Bolsheviks to act merely as equals and not as a party of dictatorship issuing orders from above.

Against any such democratic procedure the Bolsheviks struggled with all their might, and they utilized a favorable situation to dissolve the Constituent Assembly. This blow they struck not against a czarist, aristocratic, bourgeois or "white guardist" counter revolution but against the other Socialist parties, who had been more successful than the Bolsheviks in the struggle for the soul of the workers and peasants.

Hence, the abolition of all democratic rights of masses, ergo the terror. It was the necessary consequence of the rule of a minority over the great majority of the people. Hence, the fact that the terror has been indispensable for the Bolsheviks not only in the civil war but throughout the years after its conclusion. They resort to terror not only as a means of repelling counter-revolution but as an instrument of holding down and destroying all revolutionists among the workers and peasants who refuse to submit without protest to the whip of the new Red czar and his Communist cossacks.

— Reading No. 23 —

KHRUSHCHEV: *THE STALIN ERA*[23]

At the 20th Congress of the Communist Party of the Soviet Union in February, 1956, Nikita S. Khrushchev, the First Secretary of the Party and Stalin's former comrade-in-arms, corrected the pro-Stalin apologetics. He did not, however, stress the fact that the ruthless terror originated with Lenin and his overthrow of Russian freedom, nor did Khrushchev mention that the Communist Party committed greater crimes against the unhappy peoples of the USSR than Stalin committed against his fellow Communists. Nevertheless his speech (highly abridged here) presents one aspect of the most unfortunate era in modern Russian history.

✓   ✓   ✓

. . . After Stalin's death the Central Committee of the party began to implement a policy of explaining concisely and consistently that it is impermissible and foreign to the spirit of Marxism-Leninism to elevate one person, to transform him into a superman possessing supernatural characteristics, akin to those of a god. Such a man supposedly knows everything, sees everything, thinks for everyone, can do anything, is infallible in his behavior. Such a belief about a man, and specifically about Stalin, was cultivated among us for many years. . . .

Stalin originated the concept "enemy of the people." This term automatically rendered it unnecessary that the ideological errors of a man or men engaged in a controversy be proven; this term made possible the usage of the most cruel repression, violating all norms of revolutionary legality, against anyone who in any way disagreed with Stalin, against those who were only suspected of hostile intent, against those who had bad reputations. . . .

[23] The complete text of the speech with valuable annotations is available as Section Two of the *New Leader* (7 East 13th Street, New York 3, N. Y.) of July 16, 1956.

Stalin's willfulness *vis-à-vis* the party and its Central Committee became fully evident after the 17th Party Congress which took place in 1934. . . . It was determined that of the 139 members and candidates of the party's Central Committee who were elected at the 17th Congress, 98 persons, *i.e.,* 70 per cent, were arrested and shot (mostly in 1937-1938). What was the composition of the delegates to the 17th Congress? It is known that 80 per cent of the voting participants of the 17th Congress joined the party during the years of conspiracy before the Revolution and during the civil war; this means before 1921. By social origin the basic mass of the delegates to the Congress were workers (60 per cent of the voting members). . . .

The same fate met not only the Central Committee members but also the majority of the delegates of the 17th Party Congress. Of 1,966 delegates with either voting or advisory rights, 1,108 persons were arrested on charges of anti-revolutionary crimes, *i.e.,* decidedly more than a majority. This very fact shows how absurd, wild and contrary to common sense were the charges of counterrevolutionary crimes made out, as we now see, against a majority of participants of the 17th Party Congress. . . .

Now, when the cases of some of these so-called "spies" and "saboteurs" were examined, it was found that all their cases were fabricated. Confessions of guilt of many arrested and charged with enemy activity were gained with the help of cruel and inhuman tortures. . . .

When Stalin said that one or another should be arrested, it was necessary to accept on faith that he was an "enemy of the people." Meanwhile, Beria's gang, which ran the organs of state security, outdid itself in proving the guilt of the arrested and the truth of materials which it falsified. And what proofs were offered? The confessions of the arrested, and the investigative judges accepted these "confessions." And how is it possible that a person confesses to crimes which he has not committed? Only in one way—because an application of physical methods of pressuring him, tortures, bringing him to a state of unconsciousness, deprivation of his judgment, taking away of his human dignity. In this manner were "confessions" acquired. . . .

During the war and after the war, Stalin put forward the thesis that the tragedy which our nation experienced in the first part of the war was the result of the "unexpected" attack of the Germans against the Soviet Union. But, comrades, this is completely untrue. . . .

Documents which have now been published show that by April 3, 1941 Churchill, through his Ambassador to the USSR, Cripps, personally warned Stalin that the Germans had begun regrouping their armed units with the intent of attacking the Soviet Union. . . . However, Stalin took no heed of these warnings. What is more, Stalin ordered that no credence be given to information of this sort, in order not to provoke the initiation of military operations.

We must assert that information of this sort concerning the threat of German armed invasion of Soviet territory was coming in also from our own military and diplomatic sources; however, because the leadership was conditioned against such information, such data was dispatched with fear and assessed with reservation. . . .

Had our industry been mobilized properly and in time to supply the Army with the necessary materiel, our wartime losses would have been decidedly smaller. Such mobilization had not been, however, started in time. And already in the first days of the war it became evident that our Army was badly armed, that we did not have enough artillery, tanks and planes to throw the enemy back. . . . Such was the armament situation. . . .

Very grievous consequences, especially in reference to the beginning of the war, followed Stalin's annihilation of many military commanders and political workers during 1937-1941 because of his suspiciousness and through slanderous accusations. During these years repressions were instituted against certain parts of military cadres beginning literally at the company and battalion commander level and extending to the higher military centers; during this time the cadre of leaders who had gained military experience in Spain and in the Far East was almost completely liquidated. . . .

Therefore the threatening danger which hung over our Fatherland in the first period of the war was largely due to the faulty methods of directing the nation and the party by Stalin himself.

However, we speak not only about the moment when the war began, which led to serious disorganization of our Army and brought us severe losses. Even after the war began, the nervousness and hysteria which Stalin demonstrated, interfering with actual military operation, caused our Army serious damage. . . .

The willfulness of Stalin showed itself not only in decisions concerning the internal life of the country but also in the international relations of the Soviet Union.

The July plenum of the Central Committee studied in detail the reasons for the development of conflict with Yugoslavia. It was a shameful role which Stalin played there. The "Yugoslav affair" contained no problems which could not have been solved through party discussions among comrades. There was no significant basis for the development of this "affair"; it was completely possible to have prevented the rupture of relations with that country. This does not mean, however, that the Yugoslav leaders did not make mistakes or did not have shortcomings. But these mistakes and shortcomings were magnified in a monstrous manner by Stalin, which resulted in a break of relations with a friendly country.

I recall the first days when the conflict between the Soviet Union and Yugoslavia began artificially to be blown up. Once, when I came from Kiev to Moscow, I was invited to visit Stalin, who, pointing to the copy of a letter lately sent to Tito, asked me, "Have you read this?"

Not waiting for my reply, he answered, "I will shake my little finger—and there will be no more Tito. He will fall."

We have dearly paid for this "shaking of the little finger. . . ."

Let us also recall the "affair" of the doctor-plotters [in the winter of 1952-53]. Actually there was no "affair" outside of the declaration of the woman doctor Timashunk, who was probably influenced or ordered by someone (after all, she was an unofficial collaborator of the organs of state security) to write Stalin a letter in which she declared that doctors were applying supposedly improper methods of medical treatment.

Such a letter was sufficient for Stalin to reach an immediate conclusion that there are doctor-plotters in the

Soviet Union. He issued orders to arrest a group of emi-
nent Soviet medical specialists. He personally issued advice on the conduct of the investigation and the method
of interrogation of the arrested persons. He said that the
academician Vinogradov should be put in chains, another
one should be beaten. Present at this Congress as a delegate is the former Minister of State Security, Comrade
Ignatiev. Stalin told him curtly, "If you do not obtain
confessions from the doctors we will shorten you by a
head."

Stalin personally called the investigative judge, gave
him instructions, advised him on which investigative methods should be used; these methods were simple—beat,
beat and, once again, beat. . . .

When we examined this "case" after Stalin's death,
we found it to be fabricated from beginning to end. . . .

Some comrades may ask us: Where were the members
of the Political Bureau of the Central Committee? Why
did they not assert themselves against the cult of the
individual in time? And why is this being done only
now? . . . Attempts to oppose groundless suspicions and
charges resulted in the opponent falling victim of the repression. This characterized the fall of Comrade Postyshev.

In the situation which then prevailed I have talked
often with Nikolai Alexandrovich Bulganin; once when
we two were traveling in a car, he said, "It has happened
sometimes that a man goes to Stalin on his invitation as
a friend. And, when he sits with Stalin, he does not know
where he will be sent next—home or to jail." . . .

One of the oldest members of our party, Klimenti
Yefremovich Voroshilov, found himself in an almost
impossible situation. For several years he was actually
deprived of the right of participation in Political Bureau
sessions. . . .

Let us consider the first Central Committee plenum
after the 19th Party Congress [1952] when Stalin, in his
talk at the plenum, characterized Vyacheslav Mikhailo-
vich Molotov and Anastas Ivanovich Mikoyan and suggested that these old workers of our party were guilty of
some baseless charges. It is not excluded that had Stalin
remained at the helm for another several months, Comrades Molotov and Mikoyan would probably have not
have delivered any speeches at this Congress [1956]. . . .

A SELECTED BIBLIOGRAPHY

A general treatment of the various aspects of the development of modern Russia can be found in the following recently published books:

Michael T. Florinsky, *Russia, a History and an Interpretation,* 2 vols. (New York, 1953)

Hans Kohn, *The Mind of Modern Russia. Historical and Political Thought of Russia's Great Age* (New Brunswick, New Jersey, 1955)

D. S. Mirsky, *A History of Russian Literature,* ed. by Francis J. Whitfield (New York, 1949)

These three books contain bibliographies in their various fields. Professor Warren B. Walsh offers in his *Readings in Russian History* (Syracuse, New York, 1948) a handy compilation of primary and secondary source material.

Some of the specialized studies which the student will find useful are listed below:

Nicholas Berdiaev, *The Origin of Russian Communism* (London, 1937)

Sergius Bulgakov, *The Orthodox Church* (London, 1935)

William Henry Chamberlin, *The Russian Revolution, 1917-1921,* 2 vols. (New York, 1935)

John Shelton Curtiss, *The Russian Revolutions of 1917* (an Anvil Book, 1957)

————, *Church and State in Russia. The Last Years of the Empire, 1900-1917* (New York, 1940)

Sidney Hook, *Marx and the Marxists, the Ambiguous Legacy* (an Anvil book, 1955)

Hans Kohn, *Pan-Slavism, Its History and Ideology* (Notre Dame, Indiana, 1953)

Andrei A. Lobanov-Rostovsky, *Russia and Asia* (New York, 1933)

Thomas Garrigue Masaryk, *The Spirit of Russia, Studies*

in History, Literature and Philosophy, 2 vols. (New York, 1955)

Anatole G. Mazour, *The First Russian Revolution, 1825; the Decembrist Movement, Its Origins, Development and Significance* (Berkeley, California, 1937)

——, *An Outline of Modern Russian Historiography* (Berkeley, California, 1939)

Paul Miliukov, *Outlines of Russian Culture,* ed. by Michael Karpovich, 3 vols. (Philadelphia, 1942)

Bernard Pares, *The Fall of the Russian Monarchy. A Study of the Evidence* (New York, 1939)

Eugene Pyziur, *The Doctrine of Anarchism of Michael A. Bakunin* (Milwaukee, Wisconsin, 1955)

Geroid T. Robinson, *Rural Russia under the Old Regime* (New York, 1932)

David Shub, *Lenin. A Biography* (Garden City, New York, 1948)

Leonid Strakhovsky, *Alexander I of Russia* (New York, 1947)

Hugh Seton-Watson, *The Decline of Imperial Russia, 1854-1914* (New York, 1952)

Vladimir Weidle, *Russia Absent and Present* (New York, 1952)

Bertram D. Wolfe, *Three Who Made a Revolution* (Beacon Press Reprints, 1955)

E. H. Zabriskie, *American-Russian Rivalry in the Far East. A Study in Diplomacy and Power Politics, 1895-1914* (Philadelphia, 1946)

INDEX

VAN NOSTRAND ANVIL BOOKS already published

10

70
71
72
74
75
76
77
79
83
88